A Memoir in Aerograms

A Year in Middle America

Manijeh (signature)

Manijeh Badiozamani

HALLARD PRESS

A YEAR IN MIDDLE AMERICA: A Memoir in Aerograms
Copyright © 2022 Manijeh Badiozamani   All rights reserved.

Cover Design, Photography, Typography, & Production by Hallard Press LLC

Published by Hallard Press LLC.
www.HallardPress.com   Info@HallardPress.com   352-234-6099
Bulk copies of this book can be ordered at Info@HallardPress.com

Publisher's Cataloging-in-Publication data

Printed in the United States of America   1

Publisher's Cataloging-in-Publication data

Names: Badiozamani, Manijeh, author.
Title: A year in middle America: a memoir in aerograms / Manijeh Badiozamani.
Description: The Villages, FL: Hallard Press, LLC, 2022.
Identifiers: LCCN: 20209033718 | ISBN: 978-17328561-2-7 (paperback) | 978-1-7328561-3-4 (ebook)
Subjects: LCSH Badiozamani, Manijeh. | Women--Iran--Biography. | Iranian American women--Biography. | Iranian Americans--Biography. | United States--Social life and customs. | BISAC BIOGRAPHY & AUTOBIOGRAPHY / Personal Memoirs | BIOGRAPHY & AUTOBIOGRAPHY / Cultural, Ethnic & Regional / Arab & Middle Eastern | BIOGRAPHY & AUTOBIOGRAPHY / Women
Classification: LCC E184.I5 .B32 2021 | DDC 973/.0491550092--dc23

ISBN: 978-1-7328561-2-7 (Paperback)
ISBN: 978-1-7328561-3-4 (Ebook)

DEDICATION

To the memory of
Kate and Lee McClellan
of Avon Lake, Ohio.

Fonts used in this book

Sitting with my publisher months ago planning this book, we were discussing how to differientate (1) the text of my letters (Aerograms) to my family in Tehran originally written in Farsi, (2) the text of letters to my family written (typed) in English by a variety of other people and then translated into Farsi by a person in my father's office, and (3) my (whispersed) comments and asides from today that give the real background, particularly about the cultural differences between Iran and America.

We decided to use three different fonts.

This font is Caxton Book. All of my letters to my family (originally handwritten in Farsi) are printed in this typeface.

This font is Caxton Bold. All of my current comments and explanations are printed in this typeface.

This font is Pica (looks like typewriter). All of the letters to my family typed by other people are in this typeface. Understanding that cursive in English might be more difficult for the translator, they typed everything.

I hope that this makes sense for you, the reader, and helps you to enjoy and more easily read *A Year in Middle America.*

MB

Other books by Manijeh Badaziomani

Family Tales from Tehran

One Summer in My Life
A Memoir in Short Stories

The Author's books, in print and ebook format, are available on Amazon and other popular platforms.

Do you remember "aerograms?"

Think back long before email and global instant messaging apps.
Back when people actually wrote letters with a pen, mailed them
at the post office, and then waited for days—weeks even—before
receiving an answer back by mail.

If the letter was going "overseas" by air mail, we often used
aerograms. Wikipedia describes an aerogram as "thin lightweight
piece of foldable and gummed paper for writing a letter for transit
via airmail, in which the letter and envelope are one and the
same." They were convenient, cheap, included the stamp, and
demanded respect. When an aerogram arrived in the mail, you
always opened it first.

Aerograms were easy to save, too. Just wrap an elastic band
around them and pop them in a convenient drawer.

During my year in Middle America, I wrote often to my family in
Tehran on the flimsy, light blue aerogram paper. Of course, I wrote
in Farsi, the language of Iran. But the post office did not care as
long as they could read the delivery address.

Thus, my family was kept up-to-date on my activities (for the most
part) on the other side of the world.

Aerograms are long gone—replaced by electronic mail. Faster,
cheaper, more convenient, and does not require a postage stamp.
But I miss the aerogram and that personal touch of connecting
with family and friends with a pen on paper.

MB

Table of Contents

Prologue

The year is 2003, and I'm in my father's old office going through his papers. He passed away in March of 2001 in Tehran, Iran. My mother has charged me with the task of clearing his office, which she has not touched in two years!

I come across a large, faded, light-blue-covered folder. The cover is so faded it looks almost grayish, and it is held together with a white ribbon which has turned yellowish. I put the folder on his desk, pull up a chair, and untie the ribbon. Suddenly, to my disbelief and amazement, I see my own letters which I had written to my parents during my exchange student high school year in the United States in 1961-1962. My father had kept all those letters, dated and numbered them according to when he had received them. I also find three post cards which I mailed to them from Milan, Copenhagen and New York, on the way to my final destination in Ohio.

*****

My father was in the habit of meticulously keeping all correspondence—letters and telegrams, work related or personal—throughout his entire life. I don't think he ever threw away any pieces of paper that he deemed important.

Immediately, I recognize I have truly discovered a personal treasure. How often can we get a chance to go back to when we were seventeen, and look into our own thoughts, actions, and how we perceived the world at the time?

I had spent the academic year 1961-62 in America as an exchange student. The experience was so unique and new to me that I shared everything I saw, heard, and did with my family back in Iran. I wrote to them two or three letters a week—and my father had kept them all. I was the first member of my family to travel abroad.

The letters I sent to Iran reflected the impressions of a sheltered seventeen-year-old girl who left home for the first time to live in a foreign land, and the adjustments she had to make. More than sixty years ago, ordinary Iranians didn't know much about life in the United States. Neither were many Americans familiar with life in Iran. Besides, in 1961 the relationship between the two governments of Iran and the United States was totally different from what it is today. What a juggling act it must have been for that young girl to adapt and to adjust to a new way of life, gain new experiences, yet try to uphold the tradition and values of the old country, adhere to the expectation of her parents, and be a good-will ambassador all at the same time.

Now I was reading my own letters of more than half a century ago, and entering into the mind and thinking of my younger self. It was fascinating to get a glimpse into the thought process, attitude, diplomacy, and dilemmas of this teenage Iranian girl who was living in a small town, U.S.A. The letters were, of course, written in Farsi. I bundled them up and into my suitcase they went for the trip back to the United States.

Introduction

On May 22, 1961 I received a letter via United States Information Service (USIS) in Tehran, Iran informing me that I had been awarded the American Field Service Scholarship to study for a year in the United States. The letter was signed by Stephen Galatti who was the Director General of the American Field Service International Scholarship. They were headquartered in New York City, on East 43rd Street.

American Field Service (AFS) was a private organization without religious or political affiliation. It was founded in 1914 and its purpose in giving this scholarship was to further good will and understanding among nations. Iran participated in this program for the first time in 1958 by sending six Iranian students to study in the United States for a year. I was among the fourth group of Iranian students to participate in this program—eighteen of us were accepted. I was to live with a selected American family and attend high school as a senior for one year.

As a well-protected seventeen-year-old daughter of a traditional Iranian family, I had never travelled without my parents. I had attended "all girls" schools throughout my education. Culture and tradition of the time frowned upon dating and mingling with boys, or God forbid, having a boyfriend! It was extremely important to follow the society's rules, abide by family tradition, and uphold one's dignity and good reputation. And that was 61 years ago.

The American family hosting me for a year lived in Avon Lake, Ohio, and I was to attend Avon Lake High School as a senior.

Community of Avon Lake had participated in the AFS program for the first time in 1960 by hosting a Norwegian boy, and I was their second exchange student, coming from Iran.

******

It is July 1961 and I'm aboard Alitalia Airline, flying from Tehran to Milan, Italy. It is my first time flying out of Iran. Actually, I'm the first person in my family to ever travel abroad. My protective parents reluctantly have agreed to this trip. Hard to believe Dad actually agreed to let me leave home. My younger sister, Jaleh, is eleven years old. I'm not nervous at all, but truly excited for the opportunity and ready for new experiences.

I write a post card to my parents while on the plane and intend to mail it from Italy.

Dear Mom & Dad,

Hello! I'm very well, and so far have had a good time. I've had lunch on the plane and am now resting. We had short stops in Athens and Beirut. It's going to be a long day. I'm sitting next to Nahid (another AFS student) and an American gentleman is sitting to our left. We are telling him all about Iran. I have recorded everything in my notebook. The food on the plane is small portion, but delicious. I've eaten whatever I was served. Breakfast was excellent: cold cuts, milk and coffee, jam and bread. Give my love to everyone.

I must let my parents know that I'm physically fine and that I'm not a finicky eater.

We stay in Milan two days. I send them another post card. A week before I left Iran, my father had an accident. In a hasty motion he stuck his head out the window of his office on the third floor to yell instructions to his chauffeur, not realizing the window was closed. He ended up with several stitches on his forehead.

Dear Mom & Dad and Sweet Sister,

Hello! Hope you are all well. How is the cut on Dad's forehead? I'm currently in Milan, will fly to New York on Friday morning. I'm sitting at a café with Shohreh (another AFS student). We walked through the streets of Milan and took some pictures. Slept well last night and am feeling excellent. Nobody understands Farsi and no one speaks English—we've learned a few Italian words. Yesterday was a very long day and I went to bed at 8:30 p.m. Milan is very similar to Tehran, not much difference, only they have trams.

Last night Laroodi (one of the AFS boys) was sulking at the dinner table. He appeared to have been crying! He said he didn't like the food! An Italian boy carried my suitcase up to the room, and Laroodi carried my overcoat. Last night some of the kids went out to enjoy the night life. I preferred to sleep so I could get up early and go sight-seeing in the morning—they were still in bed as I left.

Regards to Uncle Jafar, Aunt Mehri, the kids and the rest.

I refuse to change my watch to the local time because I want to know exactly what time it is in Tehran and imagine what my family is doing. It is my first time eating spaghetti. The waitress shows us how to use a spoon and wrap the long noodle around the fork. We have a hard time doing it, but we giggle as we eat. Laroodi has the hardest time, he can't do it and hates the food. I think he only eats bread!

We fly from Milan to Rome and a chartered SAS plane takes all of us, plus the Italian and Swiss AFS students, to Denmark. Another post card mailed from Copenhagen.

Dear Mom, Dad, Sister, Uncle Jafar, and Aunt Mehri,

Greetings to all. We are at the Copenhagen airport. It is cold and we are all wearing our coats. I'm doing really well and you don't have to worry about me at all. On the SAS plane, we mingled with students from Italy and Switzerland. They were singing and dancing—it was so much fun on the plane. (**Our stop in Milan was 2½ days.**) Most kids bought shoes and handbags. I didn't need anything, but spent money on bananas and ice-cream! Oh, they just called us on the loudspeaker, we've got to go. Bye!

Just the mention of "cold weather" in Copenhagen, would drive my parents to worry that I might catch a cold. I have to assure them that I'm fine. Scandinavian students also join us on this charter flight to New York. America, here we come!

******

We land in New York City and are taken to an AFS building on 42nd Street. It is like a simple youth dormitory. We are to stay in New York City a few days before we are off to our final destination in different parts of the United States, to families who are hosting us. This dorm has common showers, and the food is meager and not good. Poor Laroodi; he does not eat anything, but hoards bread—that is all he eats. He takes all the leftover pieces of bread and hides them in his pocket for later.

I was awarded this scholarship based on several interviews, my academic grades, letters of recommendation, and knowledge of the English language. But the academic English I have learned is different from rapidly spoken English by the natives in NYC. I understand a little, and am not fluent in speaking. A tour of the Empire State Building, and a boat ride around the Statue of Liberty are scheduled for all of us. Alas, I'm young, and everything is so new and different that I do not pay much attention, and don't fully understand the historical significance of these two attractions.

Chapter One

August 5, 1961

Dear Parents and Sister,

I hope you are all well, and Dad's forehead is healing. I'm also hoping you have received the postcards I sent you from Rome and Copenhagen. We left for New York on a chartered SAS plane on Friday. Italian and Swiss students were with us on the plane, all singing and dancing. It was truly lots of fun. We all became instant friends. We had a stop in Copenhagen for two hours and then a stop in Canada for about half an hour. Both places were cold. I gave the yellow sweater to Nahid and the white one to Shohreh to wear, and used the overcoat myself. I offered some pistachios and almonds to the Italians, and then a flood of chocolates and candies came my way! I was surprised to see plenty of fresh fruit in Milan, huge plums and peaches. One afternoon we used the bus fare to buy peaches instead of going sightseeing around town. All the kids preferred eating the big juicy peaches. I also bought a huge banana.

We arrived in New York at 7:30 a.m. All the girls are housed in
the American Field Service Building, and the boys are in another
building. **(It is possible the boys might have been in the same
building, just on a different floor—I didn't know.)** After going
through the customs, I saw Mr. Galatti. He is 65 or 70 years old
and a super kind person. AFS representatives guided us every step
of the way. They are kind and concerned. On the plane, I rested my
head on the tray in front of me to sleep. Immediately Miss Kathy,
the AFS chaperon, came over and asked if I was okay. Told her I
was fine, just trying to nap.

As I write this, we've had lunch, and dessert was a bowl of
strawberries. Lunch was hotdog made of pig meat. I didn't eat it.

This place is like a huge dormitory with lots of beds and chairs.
Our names are attached above the beds. An Italian girl has her
bed next to mine. We'll stay here two days and then will go to our
assigned families. We are on the 4th floor and there is a bathtub
and several showers.

Mom, don't worry about me. I'm feeling just fine. There is a group
of Italian girls sitting around me right now, watching me write this
letter. They are surprised at the script and that I'm writing from
right to left. They are asking questions about Iran.

There is a piano, a television and some book cases, like a tiny
library, on this floor. At 3 p.m. I'm supposed to go for an interview
with an American lady—all the students have such interviews
scheduled at different hours.

Shoes were cheap in Milan, but I didn't want to spend my money,
and frankly didn't need anything either. Well, it is almost 3 p.m.
and I must go. Greetings to the whole family.

Your daughter,

Manijeh

Getting used to food made of pork must have been a major change at this point. On the back of this aerogram—that is what I used most of the times to write letters to my parents—I see a handwritten note by my father: *"This letter arrived at the post office at 12 noon on August 8, and delivered to the house on the same day, at 3 p.m. The action of the mailman is worthy of praise."* **Most probably my father had either sent a thank-you note to the post office, or tipped the mailman!**

August 8, 1961

Greetings to my Dear Parents.

On Monday morning about 9:10 a.m. I boarded the bus to Ohio. My co-traveler was an Italian boy named Iano. He was also coming to Cleveland. He spoke very little English and was mostly quiet, which was a blessing! We arrived in Cleveland at 11:30 p.m. On the bus we met three American girls who were kind to us, and even treated us to ice cream.

In Cleveland, my family was waiting at the bus station. You might be surprised, but they don't exactly look like their pictures! Tom and Ted are shorter, and Jane is really young. It was midnight that we arrived at the house. At the bus station they all carried my hand bag, overcoat, and suitcase.

The family has a black and red big car **(Must have been a Station**

Wagon) and a smaller car which the father drives. We made a stop and had some coca cola. They showed me different parts of the house. It is a nice two-story white house. I have a small room on the second floor which has a bed and a dresser. Jane hugged and kissed me. They also have a huge backyard. Last night by 2:00 a.m. I could not fall asleep. I was really hungry. I told Kathy, and we both went downstairs. They brought me some melons and crackers, and we all started eating and laughing.

I woke up at 7:00 a.m, hung up my clothes in a tiny closet, picked up the gifts I had brought for the family, and came down for breakfast: orange juice, milk, coffee, cereal—like our own corn flakes—bread and butter. They seemed to be pleased with the gifts. We had a lot of phone calls today, and a few ladies stopped by to visit and meet me. They were friendly and gave me a hug. The local newspaper here had already printed my picture and some write up—they kept a copy for me.

A funny but embarrassing episode happened on this first day. Last night I saw Mr. McClellan, the father of the family, for the first time while they all came to pick me up at the bus station in Cleveland. He had left the house for work before I woke up. In the middle of the day, along with other visitors, a gentleman stopped by, smiling at me broadly. I rushed to him and said, "Hello Daddy!" He was the milkman who had come in to meet the new exchange student to Avon Lake! **(My own father always came home for lunch; I assumed my American father did the same!)**

The host family for the Italian boy who travelled with me is in California on vacation. They were not at the bus station. On top of that, his suitcase got lost. I guess later on, they found it. Iranian students generally spoke better English than Italian students.

Today, Mrs. McClellan asked if I would eat pork. I explained the reason we do not eat pork in Iran is because they are not sanitary and the meat is not healthy. She said they raise the pigs in sanitary conditions here and its meat is very good. I said in that case I'll ask my parents. So, give me your response, I'll be waiting.

Please know that everyone is caring and I'm having a good time. New York was cloudy, but not cold. Here it is sunny, but humid, similar to the Caspian Sea area. On the way to Ohio, everything was green. On our last day in New York we went to see the Statue of Liberty in Manhattan.

Looking forward to your letters.

Manijeh

Mr. & Mrs. McClellan, my host parents for the year, had four children. Kathy, a junior in Avon Lake High School, Ted and Tom in 9th and 7th grade respectively, and Jane in 4th grade. I became the oldest child of the family to be enrolled as a senior in high school. Mr. McClellan worked for the United States Steel Corporation in Lorain, Ohio, and Mrs. McClellan was a homemaker. When they made application to host a foreign student, they indicated, "We feel this is an unequaled opportunity for our family to help further mutual understanding between some foreign country and the U.S.A."

To them, "the mutual part" was very important—not only others learn about Americans, their beliefs and way of life, but also for the Americans to understand others. The family

believed that a peaceful world cannot be achieved by thinking
the American way is the only way—that through this program
they have much to learn as much as to teach.

I was the fortunate one to be placed in this family, and thus
began a memorable year in my life that changed everything.

August 8, 1961

Dear Mom and Dad and Sister,

Hello! I hope you are all well. I have not received any letters from
you yet and I'm terribly worried. As I write these, I'm sitting on a
swing under the apple tree in the backyard. My two brothers are at
the end of the yard building something. Mom is in the kitchen and
Kathy is resting in her room. Green grass extends everywhere as
far as I can see. Jane and her friends, a group of cute blonde little
girls, are at another corner playing. Kathy, Mom and I just came
back from grocery shopping. Kathy did the driving, Mom and I sat
upfront next to her. I saw huge bananas at the store—I can't even
explain how big they were! The minute they saw my excitement
over the bananas, they bought a bunch.

**At the time, bananas did not grow in Iran, and they were
usually imported from Lebanon. They were tiny ones,
considered exotic fruit, and were a bit pricy! I literally went ape
over the bananas in the store!**

Goodness gracious, eight pairs of eyes are watching me as I write
this letter; I keep smiling and writing! Writing from right to left is
strange to them!

The family members liked the gifts I brought them. Any visitor who comes to the house, they immediately show them the photos, particularly the photo of Uncle Jafar with the Shah and the Queen. The local paper here also printed an article about me with photos, etc. I have saved a copy.

We went to Lorain, a town near Avon Lake—the children were in a swim competition, and they won, so everyone was happy. I watched Kathy and Jane participate in a water ballet. They kept introducing me to the others at the pool. Some called me 'Mimi," some pronounced my name "Mani-gee" or "Mani-geh"—I heard so many different strange names that I'm about to forget my own name!

Yesterday, finally I understood what poor Mr. Laroodi was going through! Change in food! No matter what I ate, I kept feeling hungry, nothing filled me up. In the morning I had orange juice, milk, toast with butter and cereal with milk. But then at the pool, I was so hungry I could cry! They brought me some milk and coffee!

Last night after I washed my hair, they let me use Kathy's hair dryer so I won't catch a cold. Yesterday Mom washed my clothes and ironed them. I thanked her profusely, and she said it is part of her job. Today, I ironed my own clothes. Things are easy here because they have all the facilities. Clothes are washed in a machine, and then put in a dryer, and if it is a bit damp, it is very easy to iron them.

Back in Iran, we had a wash lady who came to the house weekly, and did the laundry by hand, and hung them outside to dry in the sun—homes did not have washer or dryer at that time.

Yesterday, the AFS representative (liaison), a very nice lady, came

over and took me for a ride. On the way, she mentioned that
several families wanted me to spend the year with them. Therefore,
if there is any problem with the family I'm in, I should let her
know. I only thanked her.

Just now a lady came to pick up her son who is a friend of Tommy.
They call her Aunt Gloria. She loves it when I also call her "Aunt
Gloria." When I go places with Mom, I stay on the side and let her
get in first. She tells Kathy I'm a very polite girl.

I gave a picture frame and a bracelet to Kathy. Jane immediately
put Jaleh's photo into that frame and it is on the mantel piece.
Oh, my goodness, right now the boys are listening to an Iranian
song on the record player, while sitting on the floor looking at the
picture books of Shiraz and Isfahan.

Expecting letters from you soon. Greetings to the whole family.

Manijeh

**Isfahan and Shiraz are two historically significant cities in
Iran. With their beautiful mosques, monuments and gardens,
they remain two most tourist attractions in the country.**

August 15, 1961

Greetings Mom and Dad.

Hope you are well. Why don't you write to me? That is my only
concern. Every day I walk to the mailbox but there is no letter from
Iran. The entire post office workers are waiting for a letter to arrive
from Iran!

Yesterday, I received my first piece of mail from Svein-Erik, the Norwegian exchange student who was here last year. He advised me not to expect much, and to be cheerful. I'm really having fun here. Life here is the typical middle class in America. There is no luxury. I've learned how to ride a bike and play a little tennis. Every family I've visited has a ping pong table, so I get a chance to play.

Went to see a water ballet in which Kathy, Jane and Mr. McClellan were participating. Of course the men's water ballet was a comedy show, very funny. Last Saturday we were invited to a wedding at church. I was introduced to so many people, and heard so many names—very confusing. The parents of the groom took a lot of picture of me. Every day a few of my classmates come to visit me, or take me out. My coming here has created a lot of hustle and bustle and excitement in this family.

The weather changes a lot. It is cooler in the morning and warms up by noon. In short, I'm always carrying a sweater with me. Ted had a fever today and is now sleeping upstairs. Tommy, the younger brother, is gone to Boy Scouts camp. After finishing this letter, I'm going to visit one of the parks.

The kids are not as good in volleyball and ping pong as I am. I have not swum here yet—they all know the reason: it is too cold for me. I'm used to swimming in a much warmer weather.

A few days ago, we visited a young couple who just had a baby girl. They had lived in Iran for two years and knew a few Farsi words and sentences. They gave me a bottle of perfume and said it was "pishkeshi," gift. (**Pat and George Forner were missionaries in Iran.**)

I bought a pair of tennis shoes—that is what girls wear all the time, whether they go to a movie, party, or to school. They only wear high heels to formal parties or to church. On Sunday I went to church with my family. They are Protestant.

Kathy and I have a good time together, and laugh a lot. Last night we visited a friend of the family; they have two boys our age, and wanted to show us the rest of the house. One of the boys offered me his arm to walk around. I said there was no need and that I could walk by myself. They thought it was hysterical. The father of the boys said, "Great, you are a bold and daring girl coming to Avon Lake." Frankly, I didn't understand what was so daring about what I said!

Oh, I have to tell you about the wedding cake. When they cut the cake at the reception, people could take their pieces home on a napkin. I was told it is a custom that they put the cake under the pillow at night and whatever man they dream of, will be their future husband! It was funny and surprising to see an old 70-year-old woman taking the cake home with her! (**She looked old to me at the time. But now, God forbid, I don't consider 70 to be old at all!**)

Please rest assured I'm having a grand time. I get up around 9:30 in the morning. There is pineapple, orange juice and banana, jam and butter and assortment of cereals. My only request is that you write me soon and tell me what is going on in Tehran. My family likes the photo of me in the *Etelaat'e Banovan*, "Women's Magazine," and my mother shows it to all her friends.

Please, for God's sake, reply to this letter soon. I'm waiting.

Your daughter,

Manijeh

August 17, 1961

Hello Dad,

I'm overjoyed. I just received Uncle Jafar's letter. Early this morning the local post office called and said a letter from Iran has arrived. Mom and I didn't wait for the mailman to deliver it—we drove to the post office and picked up the letter. Now I'm in a really good mood, and not worried about you.

Yesterday morning I went to high school to select my courses. I think I chose well. The principal said he doesn't think I will learn shorthand. I said it doesn't matter, if after a month, I could not learn it, I'll change to a different subject. I wrote Uncle Jafar in detail about the subjects and classes. Since he is travelling up north, I mailed the letter to his Alborz High School address.

There are two courses required for getting a diploma: either American Government, or American History. Most returnee students had advised us not to take U.S. History as it is very difficult. So, I chose American Government. I guess the purpose of us coming to the U.S. is to learn about America and its government, and its people. The principal said the course qualifies me to receive a diploma. He wanted me to sign up for the U.S. History also and said it is about world history as well, like Egypt, Iran, Greece (East and West). But I mentioned that I have studied those in my school. I really prefer to spend the time learning shorthand (something new) and not to repeat the history that I already know.

I was determined to learn shorthand and typing—two classes my high school in Iran did not offer. My major was "Sciences" and learning to type was important to me. Besides, I figured

knowing those skills will help me to get jobs in bilingual offices back in Iran.

A girl in my class invited me and two others to lunch at her house. Afterward we played some kind of a game, and I don't remember its name! **(I think it was a game of croquet.)**

My older brother is running a fever and is still in bed. Younger brother is at the Boy Scout camp; we visited him yesterday at the camp. Next week, Kathy and I are going to a Girl Scout camp; I think it is in Pennsylvania. I had a roll of film printed—three photos didn't come out, but the rest were fine. It cost me three dollars.

I was dreaming of Homa and Aziz a few nights ago. Hugs and kisses to both of them.

Aziz was my father's widowed Aunt and Homa was her daughter. They both lived with my family. Aziz is the subject of several stories in my first book, *Family Tales from Tehran*.

Please tell Jaleh to continue studying English. Jane is much too young, so I will find another person to become her pen pal.

Dad, it is important for you to know that there is no drinking or smoking in this house. My American Dad does not smoke and he does not drink. He takes the photos I have brought to his work place and shows them to his friends. They are an average middle-class family, I'm comfortable here, and you can be assured that your daughter will not change. A family friend with small children invited us for dinner. My Mom was boasting about my polite behavior! The hostess turned to me and said, "Mimi, maybe you can be a role model for my children so they learn good manners and etiquette." I really don't like it when they call me Mimi!

If it is not too much trouble, I want you to get me a subscription to *Etelaat'e Banovan,* "Women's Magazine."

Sending greetings to your staff, and please thank them for me.

Manijeh, the daughter who will never forget your advice.

Etelaat'e Banovan was the first Iranian women's magazine. A young Iranian reporter, Pari Abasalti, had interviewed and wrote an article about me which was published before I left Iran. Interestingly, roughly around 2016, a TV program in Tehran called *Manoto,* had a segment named *Tunnel e zaman,* "Tunnel of Time." The host of the program had referred to that article, and talked about me on the air, wondering where in the world this girl is now and wished her the best in whatever she is doing! A cousin who watched that program in Tehran told me about it and I think somebody recorded it! I guess the article of 1961 was old enough to be mentioned in "Tunnel of Time!"

August 18

Dear Mom, Dad, Aunt Mehri and Sister,

Am extremely happy because I just received two letters from you. Last night I dreamed that Mom and Dad got into an argument and then Mom came to America to take me back to Iran. I was sobbing so much in my sleep that I woke myself up! Your two letters have cheered me up and it is a good day.

Lunches here are not big because they eat the main meal in the evening. For lunch, they put cold meat on the table to make sandwiches. I've eaten pig meat only once; they call it Ham. I don't care for it much, but I have had hotdogs and have no idea if it has pork meat. Today is Jane's birthday and I decorated her cake by writing on it, in Farsi, "Happy Birthday Jane." They found it interesting.

Mom, I bought a white blouse on sale for $2. Usually, I just look and feel the material, but today I bought! I didn't know I was so frugal in spending my money!

This afternoon we will drive to Michigan and will stay at the home of Mr. McClellan's parents. I'm taking some hostess gift for them. Yesterday, Lorain Newspaper called and then sent a photographer to take my picture. I made myself presentable, had the photo taken, and then went to a party for the girls in my class. All the girls circled around me and were asking lots of questions. Their questions were mostly about boys and girls in Iran and their relationship. I had to explain our customs. The most interesting part was the palm reading. All the girls extended their hands, wanting me to read their palms. So, like Mr. Sohrab, I put something together, pretending to tell their fortune. But at the end I told them not to believe any of it, that it was all for fun.

Mr. Sohrab was a gentleman from India my parents knew— he was also related to my Aunt Tooran. He usually did palm reading at parties.

Mom asked about my language ability. On the plane, a student from Switzerland was surprised and asked where I had learned English. The Italian kids generally were not good at speaking English. I'm pretty okay. If the conversation is not rapid, then I understand most of it.

Sometimes when I play with Lady, the family's Collie dog, I use a different accent, which Kathy finds it extremely funny! I guess I'm a good source of entertainment for the family. When I play ping pong with my brothers, I always win! Today, I sent a letter to Mrs. Parineh. My Dad just came home; I must set the table for dinner, and after we eat, we will head for Michigan.

Love to all,

Manijeh

Mrs. Parineh was my gym teacher in high school; she made sure the girls were involved in playing basketball, volleyball and ping pong. I had to boast a bit to my parents, and I was sure they would relay the information to Mrs. Parineh!

August 20th, 1961

Hello, Honorable Dad,

I read your letter twice, very carefully. Thank you very much. Thank God for having a father like you, and a kind and patient mother. I owe both of you a lot. It is the way you raised and trained me that makes me see everything in a positive light, and feel comfortable here, as if I'm in my own home. Truly, I'm surprised at myself for having adjusted so well. Nothing annoys me. The folks here are also surprised at how everything is going smoothly for me and how quickly I've adjusted.

We returned from Michigan and I immediately went to the mailbox. Thank you for your letter!

In Michigan, we spent two nights at the home of Mr. McClellan's parents. They are cheerful old folks. Following suit, I also called them Grandma, Grandpa. I gave them a paisley table cloth and a miniature hookah, and Grandma gave me a slip. We ate lunch and dinner at the home of Mr. McClellan's brother—lots of delicious food, and we laughed a lot. Americans like cheerful and happy faces. Right from the beginning, I decided not to be a sulking, pouting, or too serious a person! I hear them say, "Mimi is a sweet gal." I really don't like to be called "Mimi."

The house of Mr. McClellan's brother is by the lake and there were two motor boats. The weather was cold, but Kathy and Tommy said they wanted to go water skiing. No one told them not to go. Here, the kids are free to make their own decision. Even if they have high fever and want to go swimming in cold water, no one stops them. Mrs. McClellan sometimes tells me that the kids have responsibilities and chores such as mowing the lawn and cleaning the yard, and she does not pay them. She said there are families who pay their children for doing these chores. Anyway, the kids went water skiing while I sat in the boat. It was a fun day.

You emphasized I shouldn't be forced to go swimming! You know me by now, and don't need to pose the question. I'm not crazy, and will not even put my toes into the pool if the weather is cloudy. I've told the family that if I catch a cold, it will last a month and a half. So, they are worried and always ask about the temperature in my room and the number of blankets I need. I have not used my swimsuit yet. Also I have not used the shorts I brought with me because they are very short. I'm using the ones Kathy gave me, they come to my knees. They do not wear short shorts here. I've improved a lot in playing ping pong, and usually win whomever I play against. Dad McClellan has been filming the family and I guess he wants to send it to you.

My own father had strong phobia about germs and catching a cold, and had instilled that fear in the family. I don't know when or where this fear had originated in him. Suffice to say, at the first sign of a runny nose, or a sneeze, I had to submit to having my temperature taken, consume Vitamin C, and Cod Liver Oil—which I hated—and made sure I added layers of clothing to keep warm.

Good news, a friend of Mr. McClellan has a Koran in English. He sent it over an hour ago via his wife. I treat this holy book with such respect that the kids are scared to touch it! I think this is the book you had told me about. It has all the "Sureh's" numbered, e.g. #7, or #65. You write me the number of the Sureh and I will read it here in English.

We left Jane in Michigan, and right now I'm at home with Kathy and my two brothers. Tommy is clowning around and is trying to get my attention! Mom and Dad went to the airport in Cleveland to meet a friend who is coming back from Canada.

Once again, I want to thank you and Mother for the way you have raised me. Please continue the same way for my younger sister— she won't be sorry and will benefit even more than I have.

People comment on how young and good-looking you two are, and that pleases me!

Greetings to Aunt Tooran and Aunt Ashraf.

Your daughter,

Manijeh

Alas, I never saved any of the letters my father sent me. His letters were usually full of sage advice—how to adjust to a new environment without losing my own sense of identity. Mother's letters usually chronicled the daily events and family news.

August 22, 1961

Dear Mom,

Here is the newspaper from May 25th. The name I have underlined is Mr. King. His position is higher than the principal of our high school. **(Mr. J.I. King was the Superintendent of the Avon Lake schools)** He was the one who helped me choose my courses. It appears that like "Banoo Khanoom" in my school, the kids respect and mind Mr. King very much.

Banoo Khanoom is one of the characters in my first book, *Family Tales from Tehran*. She was assistant principal in charge of discipline, and a stern woman.

I've been asked to give talks starting January. The first engagement is to give a talk at two parent-teacher Associations at two different schools. Apparently, wearing a costume will make the talk more interesting. If you can find some kind of a costume, please send it to me with the instructions on how to wear it. Otherwise, don't worry.

I did not wear a costume in Iran. We had the latest European fashion for clothing in Tehran. However, Iran has many ethnic groups—some nomadic tribes—with their own language and traditions and clothes, such as Kurds, Bakhtiari, Gilak, etc. The costumes are colorful, and have evolved to adapt to the weather

conditions during migration and their regions. Vibrant colors, long layered skirts, matching vests, and headscarves decorated with beads and coins would have been fun to wear during my talks; but I was born and raised in Tehran, and did not belong to any tribe. I did not own any costumes, and had never worn one!

Yesterday's paper published a picture of me and my family with a nice article. I will send you a copy.

Mom, I'm at the post office right now. If I send the newspaper via airmail, it will cost me a dollar. I will send it surface mail, and it will take four weeks for you to receive it, but I only have to pay .11 cents. You will get it at the end of September.

With Love,

Manijeh

I was most frugal with my money! AFS, sent me an allowance of $14 per month, and that was my budget to pay for aerograms, stamps, films and photos to be developed, or anything else I wanted to buy! Therefore, later, I learned babysitting was a way for girls to earn extra cash.

August 23rd

Mom, Dad, Sister, Uncle Jafar and Aunt Mehri,

Greetings to all.

Last night I trimmed my own hair, front and back. Kathy wanted me to shorten her hair. But I told her she looked better with the way it was. Mom says in the Spring I should give her a haircut.

Yesterday I rode my bike—yes, I now ride a bike—to the post office and mailed you two copies of the paper with my picture and the article. Mom, they have good pattern books here. If you want I can mail you a McCall's pattern book. They cost only fifty cents!

I think clothes are expensive here. A wool skirt costs eight or nine dollars. Of course, it was less expensive for us in Iran because you sewed and made our clothes. School will start on September 6th, and until then I won't know what kind of clothes I would need.

In Iran I wore uniform to school, and it made it a lot easier for all the students.

I have a small desk in my room, by the window; it will be easy to study. I became a member of the local library, borrowed a book on shorthand and looked through it. On Saturday, there is a big party in my honor to meet all my classmates. Then on Sunday, Mom, Kathy and I will go camping with the Girl Scouts for a week. The camp is between Pennsylvania and New York. **(The camp was at Allegany State Park).**

I normally take a nap for a couple of hours during the day here, and have a hard time falling asleep at night. I mentioned this to my Mom and she replied: "My dear, you sleep 3 hours during the day, that is why you cannot fall asleep at night!"

We used to take naps in Iran during hot summer days. Besides, concentrating and speaking in English all the time, was a bit exhausting!

So much fun is going on with the kids here right now: Kathy

is playing her trumpet—she is practicing for the school band—
Tommy is playing his cornet, and Ted is banging on a big box like
a drum! And the record player is also at full blast—wish you could
be here!

Mom, I don't have anything else to report. Aunt Gloria is going to
the post office, so I cut this letter short and will ask her to mail it
for me.

Love you all,

Manijeh

August 25, 1961

Dear folks at home, Hello!

Hope you are all well. I'm really doing great. Just finished dinner:
salad, chicken, green beans and a glass of milk. Loved the
chocolate ice cream we had for dessert!

This morning my brothers discovered a rabbit nest in the front
yard. Six little baby rabbits were in the hole. As we were talking
about the rabbits, the mailman arrived and handed me six
letters. Imagine my joy! I quickly read them all and then left for a
luncheon I was invited to. When I came back, Mom informed me
that the packages you sent have also arrived. I received all the
books. Apparently, at the post office they are all talking about me
and the number of letters I have been receiving!

Mrs. Bomberger wrote me a long letter, and advised me to keep a diary
and write in it regularly. She wants me to write to her and tell her about
what I'm doing. It was such a nice and motherly letter. She advised me

to keep asking questions because that is the best way to learn.

Mrs. Bomberger was the wife of an American advisor who worked in the Food and Agriculture Organization in Iran and they were friends of my parents. She also tutored me in English, in an informal way, as a conversation partner. I would visit her home in Tehran once or twice a month after school. We would bake cookies together, and converse in English. Mr. Bomberger was involved with the College of Agriculture and the Forestry Service. When he finished his job in Iran, his next assignment was in Philippines. Later in life, they retired in Sun City, Arizona.

Now let's go over my finances. You asked me what I need. Thank you, I don't need anything yet. I might need a pair of winter shoes, but there is no hurry. At the beginning of the month, I will receive my $14 check from AFS. I figured I can spend $6 or $7 to buy myself a pair of winter shoes like Kathy's. I was told they wear galoshes over their regular shoes not to get wet. I informed them that we do not wear such a thing in Iran. If the family buys me galoshes, I would probably leave it for them after a year. I have only $5 left from my last check; will save it until my $14 arrives. Of the nine aerograms I bought I have two left, am using one of them right now. Sorry, this is such small, tight writing—I need to economize and get more on the page. Kathy made me a muumuu, and gave me a black sweater. You reminded me to drink milk. Rest assured, we always have milk at lunch and dinner.

Regarding courses offered in high school here: there are four branches. I can mix and take courses from these branches. Short hand is part of business, and American Government is part of college prep. I'm taking both. We can choose any subject we want. I borrowed a shorthandbook from the library and have been teaching myself.

Back in Iran, the curriculum was fixed and set by the Ministry of Education, and we did not choose our courses. In my high school, we had four branches: Math, Science, Literature and Home Economics. I had chosen the Science branch.

Lucia Kessler is a classmate of Kathy and lives in this neighborhood. She plays the piano beautifully. She teaches it also and has students of all ages, eight to thirty-five years old. Oh, how I wish I could learn to play! Lucia said she will teach me, free of charge. Will think about it when we get back from the camp.

A girl named Barbara invited Kathy and me to a movie. She graduated from high school last year and apparently was the girlfriend of last year's exchange student from Norway. After the movie she treated us to ice cream, and I chose banana ice cream! She is an intelligent young woman. The movie we saw was "Parent Trap." If they show the film in Tehran, please go see it and definitely take Jaleh.

Regards to all the family members who wrote me. Uncle Jafar's jokes come in handy and make these folks laugh. Please tell Jaleh to continue with English. I'm in the process of finding her a pen pal. It is already 9 p.m. and I must shower and go to bed. But hey, I smell coffee brewing downstairs. Maybe I will go have a cup before taking a shower! What do you think?

Love to all,

Manijeh

Barbara Jenson married Svein-Erik, the first AFS student from Norway who came to Avon Lake. She and Erik lived in Bergen, Norway. She passed away of cancer in August 2016.

August 29, 1961

Hello everyone at home,

We are at camp and it is 11:45 p.m. This camping area is not just for Girl Scouts or students. People rent cabins for their families— similar to when we would go to 'Oushan Fasham!'

Areas outside of Tehran, in the skirts and valleys of southern Alborz Mountain, ideal for summer vacation.

Our group occupies three cabins, and each cabin has five beds. Five girls are in each of the two cabins, and the middle cabin is for Mom McClellan and another mother who are our scout leaders. I guess this park is somewhere in New York state (not New York City). Each cabin has a refrigerator, good lighting, etc. We girls prepare our own meals. The girls have brought with them everything: radio, electric iron, electric burners, etc. I provide the humor, and the entertainment for them! This is such an interesting sight: at night the girls put their hair up in rollers and rub all kinds of cream on their faces, then take them off.

Years later, Kathy asked me why I was spraying cologne on myself before going to bed in the cabin. I divulged the truth: my bed was right next to the electric burner where the girls did the cooking, and I could smell the odor of onion, oil, etc. So, by spraying myself with cologne, I created a bit of air freshener!

There is a beautiful lake here and the girls went swimming after lunch. I met a 22-year-old American woman who is a secretary and knows shorthand and how to type. At 8:30 p.m. there was a dance, boys and girls were mingling. I felt like a spectator and observer of events, as I don't know how to dance. They tried to teach me some, but moving the body to the music kind of looked funny to me.

Then there was some kind of tension between Kathy and Joanne over a boy they met. When we got back to the cabin and I was alone with Joanne, she confided by telling me stuff. I listened to her and advised her not to take things too seriously!

When the camp was over, three station wagons hauled us back home. I was in Mrs. Newman's car—she is the liaison for AFS. My flannel winter nightgown came in handy and kept me warm. On the way back, I chatted a lot with Mrs. Newman. I asked her what I should do if I need more money. What kind of job I can have, like babysitting, etc. She asked me weather the $14 I get from AFS is not enough. I said I didn't know and that the winter was approaching and I would need some winter clothes and that I did not want to ask my parents for money. She said she will come over one day and inspect my wardrobe to determine what I need for winter. (**When I left Iran, I brought with me mostly summer clothes, and one winter overcoat, and gifts for my American family.**)

She said I should not spend my time here to earn money, and that I had more important things I needed to do. Said they will take care of my clothing needs.

That is about all to report. Regards to the whole family. Jaleh should continue with English.

Mom, tell me about your sewing classes, and if you need pattern books, there is plenty here and not expensive either.

My mother was an excellent seamstress and made all my clothes. She also had opened up a sewing class where ladies

learned how to make patterns using a French method. She would look at a picture and would know exactly how to make that dress. Now that I think about it, she was almost like a designer. For my senior prom, I sent her a photo from a magazine and she made my prom dress and sent it to me!

By the way, when you write me, please do not address me as "Mimi." I like my own name, and prefer to be called by my real name! Although the kids call me "Mimi," the grownups have started addressing me by my real name.

Jaleh should definitely have additional English lessons; please get her a tutor. When she is in high school, English will be part of the curriculum, and by then she will have a head start. She certainly has the interest and the aptitude for learning.

Manijeh

Chapter Two

September 6, 1961

Greetings to you from a faraway place! First, I'm writing in very tiny letters to economize the space. Second, I wanted to experience the first day of school and then write about it to you.

Yep, I started school today, attending Avon Lake High School. Most interesting. Each period is 35-40 minutes. We have eight periods and are constantly changing classes. The teachers are stationary and it is the students who move around.

It was totally the opposite in Iran. Students had a fixed classroom, and it was the teachers who rotated and went to different classrooms.

In the middle of the hallway, in big letters, there is a banner that says, "Manijeh, Welcome to Avon Lake." Teachers are nice to me and every time a class is over, an elderly lady who works in the school office directs me to the next class. I eat lunch at the school cafeteria, and AFS pays for my lunch. My Mom said since it is the first day, the cafeteria might ask for money, therefore she gave me some money to pay for lunch. But they did not charge me. Shorthand class seems to be a bit easy because I prepared myself for it. My classes are: study hall, speech, American Government, physical education, then lunch. After lunch, I have singing—Girls Glee Club—typing, shorthand, and then English. School is over by 3:30 p.m. I get home on the bus. In the morning I also take the bus to school at 8:00 a.m.

Let me tell you about the camp. There were 400 wooden cabins and the park was in NY State. Families can rent these cabins for a week or longer. It has swimming pool, shower, tennis courts, and they showed a film one night also. It is about one to two kilometers to the lake with a beautiful view. They have small row boats on the lake. One day, Kathy, Sandy and I rented one for an hour and rowed. I bought beautiful postcards.

Prior to going to the camp, one of my classmates gave a welcome party for me and invited the entire senior class. (**In 1962, the senior class at Avon Lake High School was eighty-four students—the entire high school population was under 500.**) They gave me a charm bracelet as a gift, and had a big chocolate cake, decorated with words welcoming me.

I received an AFS pin along with my $14 monthly check. Also a letter from Mr. Galatti, who in a friendly way, wrote, "Let us know if you have any problems or questions—there is always someone here to respond to you."

Dad had mentioned something about "bathroom towels!" Rest assured, there are lots of towels in the closet next to me. Also, you are right about learning piano—I better spend the time on my studies. I can't find ethnic or tribal costumes here to buy, and there is no need to have one. In my talks, I will show the photos of such costumes.

For Thanksgiving, which is the end of November, my family plans to go to Michigan, and stay with Mrs. McClellan's sister, Aunt Mary, and her husband Uncle Jim. Uncle Jim says he knows an Iranian whose wife, Forough, teaches at the elementary school. He plans to invite them over when we are up there.

I have enough clothes and there is no need for you to send money. If it is absolutely necessary, I'll let you know.

When Avon Lake decided to participate in AFS program and sponsor an exchange student, the people raised enough funds to be able to host a foreign student for a year. Therefore, I have to be aware and dress like everyone else, eat what they eat, and blend in and be like other students—not overly dressed up, or spend too much money on stuff.

The first day of school is always exciting for everyone. But I tried to keep calm and cool—no jittery excitement, or anxiety. Received Uncle Jafar's letter; it makes me very happy to hear that you are all together, laughing and having a good time. It is the best thing in life, to be with one's family.

School gave us our text books today. I have three books: American Government, Shorthand, and English. I don't have texts for typing or speech. Poor Kathy, she has to carry six or seven heavy books, daily.

Again, Dad advised me a lot about how to pick my friends, and to be careful. Rest assured, more than I take care of myself, others are watching over me. However, this is not like Iran that as soon as you sit next to a person in the classroom, you stay there all year long. Every hour, I'm in a different classroom with different students. Moreover, one can pretty much distinguish between individuals by their behavior! Besides, I cannot just have one special friend. I'm a guest and an exchange students. They all know me, and no matter where I go, I mingle with a group around me. Anyway, rest assured!

Don't worry if I don't write you often. I will have a lot of homework to do. About the pattern books I mentioned for Mom, goodness, I didn't want you to think my mind was on fashion, etc. I was just thinking of mother's sewing school. That is why I asked if she wanted any pattern books. That is all!

I pay for these aerograms, and intend to use every bit of space in them!.

Hugs for Jaleh, Mehran and Kamran

In 1961 the population of Avon Lake was slightly over 9000, and had just become a city. I was coming from Tehran, the Capital city with a population of over 2,000,000. It was difficult for my parents to imagine life in a small community, and my father's advice was always related to perils of living in a big city!

September 9, 1961

Dear Mom & Dad and Sister,

School has been in session for three days now. We have no school on Saturday and Sunday – they take off two days. (**In Iran, I had** only Fridays off.)

Yesterday after lunch, all the seniors gathered in the cafeteria, along with some teachers. Every year they choose a class president, vice-president, secretary and treasurer. Most often, the president and vice-president are boys; secretary and treasurer are girls. They put the name of the candidates on the board, then passed pieces of paper to the students to vote. Four students were nominated for class secretary. My name was among them. When they counted the votes, I had the most votes. I guess they wanted to be nice to me! I was surprised, so were some of the teachers. The kids kept congratulating me.

I have no doubt the senior class of 1961-62 at Avon Lake High School wanted to make my year memorable and special by voting me to be part of the class officers.

I enjoy shorthand, typing and speech. But I don't understand much of the American Government. English class is hard too because it is all English literature. I need to get help in those two classes. American Government text has a lot of tough vocabulary. But that is okay, everything is tough at the beginning, am sure it will get easier slowly.

Newspapers arrive regularly, but frankly I don't have time to read them. I just look at the headlines, and am glad you got only a three-month subscription.

My parents gave me a subscription of the daily Iranian newspaper, so that I would be informed of the current events back in Iran.

Girls come to school in their regular clothes—there is no uniform.

They also use a lot of makeup.

This was in sharp contrast to my school in Iran. I wore a uniform and absolutely no makeup was allowed.

And no matter how many books they have to carry, no one uses briefcase. The girls carry purses and put their money and make-up in it—the type of purse we use when we go to parties in Iran.

My clothes are washed by the washing machine, but my delicate clothes I wash by hand because the washing machine rips them apart. Writing letters take a lot of time. I didn't want to write so soon, but wanted to let you know I was elected class secretary.

September 16, 1961

Dear loving parents,

I'm always thinking of you and your words of wisdom. When I get up in the morning, I pray to God to protect me. My aim is to act in such a way that you will be proud of me. I'm saying these words from my heart.

It is Saturday evening. This morning we visited the county fair with Aunt Gloria and her family, and had a picnic lunch there. We do not have such a thing as county fair in Iran. Saw all sorts of animals: chickens, lambs (so fat that they could hardly move), and the competition among horses to see which one could pull heavier load. Also saw varieties of vegetables, fruits, and handicrafts.

Being born and raised in the capital city, Tehran, I was not familiar with farm animals. The fair was most interesting,

including the varieties of vegetables, and their huge size.

Yesterday, Mom and Dad McClellan and I went to a welcome party for me and another girl named Pat Kaliz who is a senior in my class. She showed slides from her trip and gave a talk.

Pat was an exchange student from Avon Lake to Guatemala, and had spent the summer there through the AFS program. I was told I will be doing the same thing starting January. I remember I was watching her very carefully, and thinking where I would stand on the stage when I show my slides!

Weather has turned rather cold and I'm wearing my yellow jacket to school. Thanks for sending my long pants, I really needed it.

I wish you could see high school girls here—they use so much makeup when they come to school. The other day I saw a girl wearing a dress with thin shoulder straps. Imagine coming to school like that. Iranian girls are more modest. Some of the freedom of the students bothers me. I ask questions, but sometimes they can't answer me. Although there is a lot of freedom here for the young, they appear to distinguish between good and bad. Anyway, my job is to observe, study, eat and enjoy myself.

This segment of my letter amazes me and shows that I'm beginning to understand the differences in societies! This is actually a crucial and pivotal point in my learning experience about life in America: while the customs, and habits are different on the surface, the underlying values remain the same. Regardless of wearing makeup, or spaghetti strap dress to school, the teens can distinguish between good and bad behavior. I recognize some societies are more permissive than others.

I'm doing well in shorthand class—I was the only one who had done the homework. Our teacher, Miss Saare, made an example of me and told others that although I didn't have to learn the whole thing, I had done the work. American Government class is still difficult, but I have no choice, I have to learn it. I'm getting better in English. Mr. Turner who teaches Spanish and French, will be helping me with my studies three times a week. I'm doing fine in speech class, and received a good grade.

I couldn't believe it when back in Iran Eddie told me the girls here wear something different every day! I have only one skirt and wore it to school three times this week, but used it with different tops. I receive compliments on the blouses you have made me!

Back in Iran, I wore the same uniform day in and day out. Later in the year, Kathy and I began exchanging clothes, and that expanded my wardrobe, and no one in school knew who owned what!

Regarding finances: I have $5 left from the money you gave me in Iran. AFS sends me $14 a month. I have spent $2 on a pair of socks, hairspray and postage. My balance is now $17. I need to buy more aerograms. I won't be able to find winter shoes on sale now. We are heading toward winter and all the sale items are for summer stuff!

Regarding "driving," forget about it. AFS has strictly forbidden exchange students from driving, not even touch the steering wheel. It is a good rule as there are lots of dangers involved.

Jaleh, for you I have found a pen pal. She is the younger sister of my friend in school, Judy Fischer. Her name is Jean Fischer. Have met their mother and she seems real nice. I gave them your address and she will write you in simple sentences. But you need to work hard on English and answer her letter well.

Received Uncle Razmi's letter. Wow! What a literary specimen, in words and sentence structure, as well as his amazing handwriting!

Razmi is one of the interesting characters in my first book, *Family Tales from Tehran.*

The book you sent me, *Our Country,* has all the information I need for my talks. Please do not send any more books. I have 66 slides, and Erik, last year's exchange student, wrote and said that is enough, but important to pay attention to how I arrange them.

Love to all,

Manijeh

September 21, 1961

My dear parents, Hello!

Hope you are both well. I'm doing well, too. School starts at eight-thirty in the morning and ends at three-thirty—we have only half an hour for lunch. I've worried so much about winter and cold weather here that yesterday Mom and I went shopping and bought a pair of winter shoes for me. Now I feel relieved! It cost $6.70. The shoe clerk was surprised that I was buying winter shoes at this time. Mom explained to him that I'm not used to this climate and better be prepared soon. The weather changes quickly here. One day I wear my yellow jacket, another day it warms up. I carry a sweater with me at all times.

I've joined two school clubs here: Language Club, and Future Nurses Club (they talk about first aid, etc.) Mr. Turner helps me with my studies. Right now he is talking to my Mom about helping with scheduling my talks. I'm finding school work a bit easier, but it sure takes a lot of time to do my homework. Jean Fischer has already sent Jaleh a letter; Judy showed it to me at lunch today. It was relatively easy for Jaleh to understand. She should go ahead and write back and not to worry about mistakes. She will get better. My English has improved quite a bit.

Newspapers arrive regularly, and I have received 33 letters so far. Don't wait for me to write answers to your letters, I'm very busy, you go ahead and write. Sometimes I read Dad's letters over and over. Thanks for mailing the costume—people here ask me about "national costume" and I say "it is on its way!"

In gym class we have only 10 minutes to shower and get ready for the next class! Gym class is mandatory here—opposite of my school in Tehran, when some kids used the gym time to doodle on the board! It is great to be out in the fresh air with all the greenery around. Good exercise!

Don't have more to say. Greetings to family members.

Love,

Manijeh

September 25, 1961

Every day when I come home from school, I ask Mom McClellan if there is a letter for me. She jokingly said, "You will be spoiled if you receive letters daily!" Anyway, *Etelaat'e Banovan*, "Women's Magazine," arrived today.

Mrs. Newman, the AFS liaison, came and picked me up to go over to her house for dinner. She prepared a delicious dinner and excellent dessert. After dinner we talked—folks here like it when I talk about the differences in how we do things back home. I always tell the truth about how things are. However, the couple of books I saw in the library about Iran are old and depict ugly scenery and poverty.

I recall the local library in Avon Lake had only two old books about Iran at the time. When I looked at the photos, I was surprised and dismayed because they only showed remote poor villages in old days! I was coming from Tehran, the capital city. But I suppose those scenes were also part of Iran I had not seen.

The subject of winter clothes came up. Mrs. Newman showed me her daughter's winter clothes, which was not much different from my own. She said she will come and inspect my wardrobe and if my clothes are suitable for winter, she will write you and put your mind at ease. She invited me to visit them again.

I've asked everyone to call me "Manijeh." The nickname, "Mimi" does not mean anything. I like my own name and I think it is beautiful. Weather is crazy here, and changes a lot. One day I have to wear my yellow jacket, the next day shorts and T-shirt. Kathy gave me a nice dress which I wore to school and everyone asked if you have made it. I assured everyone it was made in the U.S.A!

In the winter the girls wear leotards, and Mrs. Newman said if I have two or three pairs of those, I will be okay with the cold. I plan to buy a couple—they cost $2 a pair.

I babysat for a family with four kids, cute and nice. I talked to the children and told them stories and they went to bed at 10:00 p.m. The lady of the house told me to feel at home and check the fridge and eat what I want. I had a glass of milk, an orange and a peach! Yum!

School is fine and I'm getting the hang of it. Dad, you said I can consult and ask you questions. Here is one. If I want to be a sociable girl and participate in school activities and be part of the group, I have to associate with boys because boys and girls all mingle in activities. Also, I get invited to a lot of places and it is not good if I don't dance with boys in my class. Although I don't know how to dance well, sometimes it is necessary. At the end of the year there will be a big dance for the senior class (those in 12th grade). They call it Prom. The write-up of last year's Prom was in the newspaper that Kathy had sent me, please look at it again and see what kind of dress the girls wear to Prom. Of course, Kathy and I do not have a Prom dress yet; it is too early to decide on that. It is in the spring, and students are selling newspapers now to save money for the Prom.

The English teacher stays half an hour after school and helps me with English literature. I have improved a lot.

It is 11:00 p.m. and I'm really sleepy. Greetings to the whole family.

Your daughter,

Manijeh

On September 29, my American Mom, Mrs. McClellan, sent a letter to my parents in Iran.

September 29, 1961

Dear Mr. & Mrs. Golbabai,

Thank you so much for your very nice letter. I had not realized, until I received it, that there would be some way in which we could communicate. If the Farsi with which I addressed this letter was good enough to reach you, then I should be able to write to you often.

We all want to thank you very much for "lending" us your daughter for a year. We feel that this is the most wonderful year in our lives. Manijeh is a beautiful and charming girl. You must be very excellent parents to have raised so nice a girl. She is very polite. I'm certain that there are things that we do that she perhaps does not approve of — but she does not criticize.

I think that her two main worries are her food and her clothes. I think she will need a warmer coat for school which we will get her. Also, we will buy her boots and gloves. She is very worried about the cold weather, but we will make certain that she always is dressed warmly enough.

In America we eat breakfast, lunch and dinner. Before going to bed we often eat something. Our children do not eat between their meals. Manijeh has explained that her stomach is small, as is her father's and grandfather's and that she must eat often. I have told her that she may eat any time she wants to. Our food is very different

from yours, but I think that in another month, she will
be more used to it and enjoy it more than she does now.

The teachers at school say that she is doing very well in
her studies. Our school is very different but she will
soon become accustomed to it. The boys and girls all like
her. She is not used to being with boys. The decision as
to how friendly she wants to become with them will be
up to her. We do not want her to do anything she does not
believe is right.

I wish that we could meet you. I feel as if I really know
you — and the uncle who jokes.

Love to all.

Kay McClellan

I chuckled, and found this letter most interesting.

True, I was constantly worried about cold weather! I grew up
in a family with a father who was constantly worried about me
"catching a cold." I never went outside with wet hair. If two
windows were open simultaneously, I had to sit away from the
air current! After a shower, I had to keep myself really warm
and wrapped up in towels. I grew up thinking catching a cold
was the worse sickness in the world! My fear definitely showed
during the first few months in Ohio.

I also chuckle about the comment she made about the food. I
did not like the food in the U.S. at the beginning. Besides, no
one fussed over me to eat the food during dinner!

The custom of "Taarof" was well and alive in my family. Taarof is a Persian word which refers to an Iranian form of civility, politeness and etiquette. Taarof is the polite refusal of the offered food, knowing the host will insist a second time! In my family it was exercised for guests as well as for family members. My parents insisted on offering food to me, or putting the food on my plate, even if I had politely refused! At the McClellan's house there was no such "Taarof." Food went around the table only once, and everyone took certain portion. I wanted to be polite and refused the food that was passed to me. To my amazement, the dish was whisked away and did not come back! It didn't take me long to figure it out. After a few nights of going hungry, I had to put aside politeness and do away with "Taarof." Today, we say, "In Rome do as Romans do!"

Back in my high school, we were assigned a fixed classroom, and the teachers rotated. Between each class I had 5-10 minutes, enough to chew on a little snack, dried fruit, candy, cookies, etc. At Avon Lake High School, I had to rush from one class to the next, no time to munch on anything. Then at lunch, I was faced with the cafeteria food! Whatever was put on my tray I had to eat. That was it. Indeed, learning to cope with the cold and the food were the two major hurdles at the beginning. Learning to go to school with boys was another hurdle—more on that later. On with another letter...

September 30, 1961

Dear Mom and Dad and Sister,

It is Sunday morning, everyone is still in bed, but I got up early to write you. Mother said she looks forward to my letter by the end of the week. Well, I look forward to your letters every day! Today, an American family from Youngstown, Ohio is coming to visit us. They are host parents to another Iranian girl, Mehri Nehmadi. Probably we will speak Farsi together and no one will understand us!

First of all, rest assured I will not be skiing here. This place is cold, but there are no mountains, but there is a big lake here (Lake Erie). Majority of my classmates, boys and girls, have jobs: sales, gas station attendant, shoe salesman, or babysitting. Anyway, they get a job to make some money, it is not to help their parents. They tell me their parents provide for their food, and clothing, and that they need to earn their own pocket money for additional expenses.

The idea of having a job while student in high school was totally new to me. I was told just to study and get good grades, and that was my job. Those my age whom I knew, within our circle of friends, relatives and family, did not work.

Back to the weather, the topic of our discussion in every letter! It has turned cold and I don't have enough winter clothes. I need to buy some wool skirts and sweaters, and it will cost me some money, and I'm not happy about that. The winter coats here have thick lining and that is what keeps them warm.

School is going well. In speech class, whatever topic I talk about is interesting for the students. Moreover, I'm not shy when I speak, smile and show a good sense of humor. The teacher, Mr. Bolen, is both fun and funny. He normally praises my talk and says my personality comes through. I'm not sure how, but I guess he knows better!

In the American government class the teacher asked a question. I knew the answer and for the first time raised my hand. Well, guess what? In the afternoon when I entered the school office, everyone praised me for having answered the question! I'm sure that is a motivator to make me work harder, and answer more questions!

I'm going to an orientation program for all the AFS students who are around here (northern Ohio). I heard there is a girl from India who had brought only a few thin Saris with her. Now that the weather is turning cold, everyone is trying to find her some winter clothes. According to Mrs. Newman, the gal is very tiny and it is hard to find something to fit her.

Kathy and I have fun together and laugh a lot. But we do not interfere in each other's business, therefore we have no problem.

You said you wanted to send me my letters of recommendation, along with my report cards. They have to be translated into English and sent through the office of the American Friends of the Middle East. It is not necessary, but it could be nice for the school administration here to have them on file.

Dear Sister Jaleh: Mom and Dad have praised you which shows you have been studying very hard. If you get a letter from Jean Fischer, make sure you answer her. I see her sister in school every day. Something interesting, I made Chelo Kabob twice **(Persian dish of rice and kabob).** The first time I messed up the rice, the pan was too small. The second time, we had eleven skewers of kabob and two platters of rice, butter added, and had Mr. & Mrs. Forner over for dinner. They had spent two years in Iran and asked me to fix this dish for them.

Okay, family members are up and I'm going to put some food in my growling stomach!

Love to all,

Manijeh

Chapter Three

October 5, 1961

Mom, Dad, Uncle, Mehri, Homa, Aziz, Jaleh, Mehran, Kamran,

(In short, all of you folks at home)

I've received your letters, and I'm replying to you all.

I had started receiving letters from friends in the U.S. and responding to all that communication, individually, was getting to be too much! Addressing all the folks in one letter, was a way to send a communal letter for all to read.

A while back, the Forners, invited me over for dinner. (The couple who spent time in Iran as missionaries). They made the rice, and had yogurt too! After dinner, Pat Forner took me shopping and bought me a warm sweater and a handbag. She also bought me a pair of shoes as birthday presents. She gave me a pretty wool skirt, and said I could borrow and wear any of her clothes to parties I'm invited to.

October 1st was the gathering of all the AFS students in a nearby town. The girls were from: Pakistan, Finland, Costa Rica, Lebanon, Norway, England and me from Iran. The boys were from: Germany, Denmark, and Argentina. We each gave a little talk. Those from Costa Rica and Argentina didn't know much English, but we all had a good time.

In my last letter I mentioned the other Iranian girl (Mehri Nehmadi) who came to visit us with her American family. We hugged and she cried. When we spoke Farsi to each other, it sounded a bit strange to our ears, and then we would laugh. My sister, Kathy, and Mehri's American sister, Jan, were present. Kathy would laugh with us, although she didn't know what we were talking about. But Mehri's sister was not jovial, would not talk or laugh. Later on, Mehri told me her American sister was very jealous of her. I'm so glad and thankful that Kathy is not jealous, and that we get along.

Changing to another subject, folks here exchange gifts for Christmas. My family is thinking of what to send you guys. If you want, you can send them pistachios for Christmas. My Dad likes pistachios and they all like Gaz that I brought.

Gaz is an Iranian nougat. It is made from the sap of the Tamarisk tree and is traditionally combined with flour, pistachios or almond pieces. Sometimes it can have a subtle rose flavor. Gaz is a favorite delicacy and much appreciated as a gift in Iranian households—usually served with tea.

I laughed so hard when I was reading Homa's letter and the stories about her students. I shared those stories with my family, so they don't think I was crazy and laughing for nothing. Also told them Homa is a math teacher. Here they respect teachers a lot. Not everyone can be a teacher.

Homa was my father's cousin. Along with her mother, Aziz, they lived with us. There are several stories about both of them in my other books.

Uncle Jafar asked me about sports and school in Avon Lake. Basketball has not started. So far, I have seen golf, baseball, and football. Funny thing is, their football is different from ours! It is football in name only, otherwise they carry the ball with their hands. I don't understand the game, but maybe later I will. Our school building is very large, maybe even larger than Alborz High School. Teachers have fixed / permanent classroom. When the bell rings, it is the students who change classes. There are lockers in the hallways; each student has one which he/she can open with combination lock. I eat lunch at school, and then by 3:30 school is over. I come home on the bus, and if I don't move fast, the bus leaves, and then I have to walk home. We had PE class today and played football. In a way it was funny, because only boys are on the football team. When I mentioned this to my fellow students, I was told that whatever game the boys play, the girls are supposed to play too. But of course I don't see any girls on the football team!

I don't have any breaks between classes, but have "study hall" once or twice a day—it is considered as break. However, we are not allowed to talk in the study hall, it is time to do our homework.

I'm having a great time here, but also await your letters. Our washing machine broke down, and Mom took the clothes to a laundry place.

Love to all,

Manijeh

October 9, 1961

Dear Mom and Dad,

Yesterday we celebrated my birthday, and I received a lot of
presents. Mrs. Newman brought me a pair of green long pants
which are lined, and a yellow knitted sweater. Mom gave me
two pairs of gloves, one for school, one for parties, and a white
beautiful blouse. I got other gifts such as cologne, earrings,
necklace, etc. Preparing the food was my responsibility. I made
Chelo Kabob. I wanted to make Halva for dessert, but didn't really
know how! It turned out to be yellow, the color of squash. I didn't
have rose water to add, so it didn't have a good taste or smell. Here
rosewater is used in the bathroom, and they laugh if I say it is
used in cooking. My mom had bought some saffron, which I added
to the top of rice. It was an interesting meal!

**I had never cooked in Iran. For the life of me, I can't figure
out why the family trusted me to prepare a meal and why
I volunteered to do so! Maybe they expected me to cook
something Persian. These days, one can find Persian Halva
recipes on YouTube. But sixty-one years ago, trying to make
something from memory—I had only watched my mother make
it—was a total disaster. And I perfectly understood when Mrs.
Newman's daughter, Janet, discreetly, was offering the tasteless
dough to the family dog, while trying to dispose of the "Persian
dessert." Fresh, seasonal fruits were usually our dessert in
Iran. Why did I choose to make Halva? I would never know!**

My birthday cake was a surprise and fun-looking. It was a small
cake decorated with a doll (with dark hair) in the middle of the
cake, and the entire skirt of the doll was made of icing with my

name written on it.

Last Saturday was a special dance at school—Homecoming dance. It was my first time attending such an event and I went with Lucia and her mother. Usually parents and teachers are present and act as chaperones. Students had voted earlier and chosen a king and queen who were introduced at the dance and were crowned. Christy was the queen and George, a football player and class president, was the king.

I now have three pairs of leotards, and lots of warm clothes. Mrs. Newman came up to my room and inspected my wardrobe, and assured me I do not need anything else. She will write you to put your mind at ease.

When I was opening all my gifts yesterday, Tom, my younger brother, said that he wants to be an exchange student, too, when he is older. They all laughed! And Kathy also suggested we exchange clothes.

Tom actually did become an exchange student and went to Uruguay with the AFS program when he was in high school.

Our music teacher (Mr. Hisey) has selected me for the Girls' Glee Club. He said I have a good voice, but that I have to pronounce the words with an American accent. The host family of last year's exchange student (Mr. & Mrs. Hoxie) invited Kathy and me to go to Cleveland with them—we saw Swan Lake ballet. It was wonderful.

Regards to the whole family,

Manijeh

October 10, 1961

Dear Mom and Dad,

The family celebrated my birthday yesterday at home. But today
students celebrated my birthday at school. Wow! One by one
they were wishing me a happy birthday. At lunch one of the girls
brought a big cake with red candles on it and they all sang "Happy
Birthday." What fun it was. I received a lot of cards, and some
gifts, including a couple of Avon Lipsticks.

**Avon cosmetic brand was well-known in Tehran, and were sold
only in exclusive stores at the time.**

Dad, you asked me to write you my thoughts on the subject. I
really don't have any particular thought, yours is as good as mine.
Please don't worry about school dances. Avon Lake is a very small
town and people basically know each other. Besides, school dances
are only for the students of this school, and teachers are also
present as chaperones. There are no strangers at these dances.
Although the behavior of the American youth is very interesting
and different from what I'm used to, nothing comes as surprise or
shock, and I do not judge. I'm in charge of my emotions and accept
things as if they are normal to me, as if I've been living in America
for hundred years! My calmness even surprises me!

**Alas, I had not saved any of my father's letters. I don't
remember why he was so worried about school dances and
presence of strangers! Come to think of it, we lived in Tehran,
the capital city of Iran with a large population—two million at
the time. My parents could not imagine how life would be in
a small town, U.S.A. Besides, as an exchange student, I was
a celebrity of sort in that community, and was guarded and**

protected at home and at school. Moreover, the watchful eyes of the AFS liaison, made sure I was safe, and I'm positive she reported to AFS headquarters in New York, if there was any problem.

You said you will be sending $40 via a friend's brother. I already wrote you that I don't need any money. On a different topic, and I hope Dad does not get upset about it. I'm learning piano from Lucia. I go to her house on Saturday mornings and she teaches me simple songs. It is a good recreation, and relaxation. When I get tired of studying shorthand and American government, I play the simple songs I have learned. It refreshes me and I go back to my studies again. Be assured, it is only once a week on Saturday morning and I don't have school on Saturdays.

It is 5:30 p.m. My Mom is at a Girl Scout meeting. Dad and the boys are hitting golf balls in the backyard. Dad just came in and said since Mom has not returned yet, he is going to start the dinner. I better go help him.

Regards to the family, Manijeh

October 16, 1961

Dear Parents and Sister,

Hugs and kisses for all.

My high school friends from Iran are writing and giving me the scoop! One gal had her appendix out, another one had a nose job done!

I'm very much involved with my school here. Am in several clubs: language, photography, future nurses, Pep club, and I'm also in the Student Council. The first period that I have study hall I work at the school library. Our school library is big, and more importantly students use the library a lot and enjoy books.

My English teacher thinks I've improved a lot. I'm healthy and you don't need to worry about me. Weather has turned cold and I use my heavy coat.

A girlfriend has invited me to travel to Pittsburgh with them next weekend (to visit her aunt). I might be able to contact Sholevar.

Mr. Sholevar was a young doctor who was doing his internship or residency somewhere in Pennsylvania. He was a relative of my father, and I knew him and his family.

Father, I want to participate in all kinds of school activities this year, that is why I have joined many different clubs. It is a good way to learn about America and American youth.

I'm sure my father was flabbergasted that I joined all those clubs. This was not the norm in my family—and for most families I knew—at the time. My parents expected me to concentrate on my studies! However, in my high school in Iran, my Persian language teacher, Mrs. Taleghany, (God bless her). formed a theater club for the interested students. I was in a couple of school plays, usually as funny characters! In my first book, *Family Tales from Tehran*, I refer to my love of writing scripts with my cousin, and then performing for the family after dinner.

I want to write to many people, but do not have the time. Some of the food here are hard for me to eat, but the desserts are always wonderful. Normally, I eat the food, whatever it is, otherwise I have to go hungry!

Till next letter, Bye,

Manijeh

October 18, 1961

Dear Father,

I received a $40 check from Mr. Fayaz's brother. I do not need any money now. AFS rule is that any time you want to send money, it has to go to their office first. Then, I'll have to write to AFS and ask for money and give the reason why I need it. Mrs. McClellan has a handbook that she refers to whenever she has a question. The handbook said: "whenever your student receives money, let us know." So, she wrote to N.Y, reported the check and Dr. Fayaz's address. I will wait and see what AFS, N.Y. says. If I'm to return the check, I will. If they have no objection, then you let me know what you want me to do with the money. As of now I have $16 and if I need to buy a skirt, I can use this money.

Tomorrow will be six weeks since school has started, and I will be getting a progress report. I will share it with you. Mom McClellan also wrote to AFS to get their permission for me to go to Pittsburgh. Wherever I want to go, it has to be approved by AFS.

Fall weather definitely has arrived, trees have changed colors and I wish you could be here to see them. They are beautiful. Nature is really pretty here—in the summer everything was green. Now they are green, yellow and red all mixed. I'm sure the winter would be all white which will have its own beauty.

I chuckled when I read this part of my letter. For a change I'm not complaining about the cold, but talk of the beauty of winter, and the possibility of snow!

So far, I've been booked for 12 speaking engagements which will start after January.

I hope you, mother and Jaleh are happy together, perhaps only missing me! I will join you in 10 months. Bye

Your very good daughter,

Manijeh

Kathy decided to write a letter to my mother in Iran, which obviously my father had also kept.

October 23, 1961

Dear Mom:

Hi, I hope you are well. Say hello to my aunt and uncle and father and sister for me. Tell them all that Manijeh and I are having a wonderful time together. We always talk together about our friends, food, music, clothes, and problems. I have been trying to teach her the American "rock and roll dances. She learns very good and fast. But she won't dance with us when we go to a dance because she feels embarrassed. I think I know how she feels. If I were in your country I think I would feel the same way.

Yesterday she got back from a visit to a little town just outside Pittsburg, Pennsylvania, with one of her girlfriends and her mother and father. From what she has told me she had a very good time. She said they ate all the time and all different kinds of food. Her girlfriend's aunt cut her hair. It looks real nice. Everybody likes it. She is looking like an American girl more everyday.

Manijeh and I laugh together all the time. We laugh about everything. Especially we laugh about the boys. This weekend we are going to a Halloween party. We are going to dress up in costumes.

We are adding another room to our house. It will be a recreation room. Dad is starting it this week. When it is finished we will have finished our breezeway into a dining room and added the new recreation room. It should be done in early Spring.

Bye Bye for now,

Love,

Kathy

October 25, 1961

There is so much to see here, and I have tons of school work, therefore I'm extremely busy. Time becomes scarce and I could not write you for a few days.

My Mom is baking a three-layered cake which is for dessert tonight. She also had a little cupcake for me as an after school snack. I had a letter from Jaleh which said you have received Mrs. Newman's letter. Apparently Mrs. Newman had said "Manijeh misses you all,"—that had upset mother." I repeated this to Mom McClellan and she said, "Write your parents that we cannot sleep at night because of you and Kathy giggling so hard and loud, and that we have to send both of you to bed by force!"

Jaleh also reported that Mother says, "If you are sad, then just come back home."

You see dear parents, when I show your beautiful photos to people around here, they ask me, "Are you sad that you are away from them?" And I answer in affirmative! Otherwise, not only I don't want this year to end, but also wish I could win another scholarship and stay here longer. Anyway, we both know that this is only for one year.

About my trip to Pittsburgh—we stayed at my girlfriend's aunt. Her aunt has a beauty shop in her basement and gave me a haircut. She did not accept any money and said I was her guest. Everyone liked it and they all say I look like an American girl. I could not visit with Dr. Sholevar, but we talked on the phone and he said hello to you all. This was a fun trip and we ate and laughed a lot.

School has decided to use S (satisfactory) and U (unsatisfactory) to evaluate my work. If all is S then that means I'm doing okay.

The AFS girl from Pakistan (Fauzia) invited me for an overnight stay—We had a good time talking about our experiences so far. Most probably I will invite her for sleepover as well. Kathy has written a letter to mother which you must have received by now.

No words from AFS regarding the $40 check. So, I'm keeping the money. Father has not written me for a while—I know he is busy too, and letter-writing takes a lot of time, and time is really valuable.

Rest assured I'm having a good time here and am very comfortable.

Nothing more to say,

Manijeh

Chapter Four

Wed. November 1, 1961

Hello Dear Father,

I just came home from school and opened your letter. I was stunned! I didn't know to laugh or cry. I'm surprised that you still don't know how I think. You are still repeating the same words of advice that you used to tell me two years ago. I'm not upset over what you write and usually read your letters two or three times.

Now, reading the rest of this letter I had written to my father sixty-one years ago, truly evoked in me, the same sad, funny, and angry feelings I felt at that time. It was very difficult for me as a teenager, away from home, and wanting to please my parents, yet realizing they had no clue about the environment I was living in. I knew their life style was different from what I was experiencing in the United States. I was trying to put into words that he should not misjudge me, that I knew who I was and that I had not let the environment change me! Yet, I had to also let them know it was important for me to behave in certain

ways that would be in harmony with my environment, and that would allow me to gain new experiences. What a juggling act, both in words and in action, that I had to go through!

I do get upset not knowing how you are judging me. If I were the type of person to let the environment have negative effect on me, I would have changed the first month. You said Mrs. Newman had written to you that, and I quote, "Manijeh does not like or approve of the freedom of the American youth."

An Iranian AFS student who is in California now, wrote me two months ago, and I'm quoting her verbatim: "The Diploma here is not worth anything, therefore, I've decided to have just fun this year, it is better than a piece of paper." And in another part of her letter she said: "I've become like a movie star, wherever I go people turn to look at me. It is good to be famous." Well, I don't know what she and others think about the experience of this year, or how they want to spend the year, but I have carved my own course of action and know how to go forward. The boys are rather afraid to come close and treat me with a lot of respect. But as I mentioned, when there is a party in honor of all the AFS students, and someone asks me to dance, it is impolite to refuse. I assure you, one-hundred percent that dancing as you know it in Iran is different from dancing in a school setting. In Iran, as soon as a boy and a girl dance together, everyone thinks they are lovers. But here, dancing is treated normally. Fathers and daughters, mothers and sons, they dance together. Of course, there are also those who are romantically attached and are considered boyfriend and girlfriend.

Anyway, your letter upsets me a lot, and I want to both laugh and cry at the same time. I'm bewildered. What do you want me to do?

There is something here called "Halloween"—everyone wears a costume and has a mask. Last night there was a Halloween dance at school where Mr. & Mrs. McClellan were the chaperones. What do you think I should have done in a situation like this? Sit at home and not participate? I'm here only for a year and Halloween party is only once. If I attend in order to learn what is going on, then I'm constantly thinking that you guys are unhappy and disapprove of what I'm doing.

Parental approval was extremely important in my family. My father basically set the tone, and his words were the rule of law, to be obeyed without question. In this letter, I'm basically challenging my father and his words.

Moreover, I want to quote from your own letter of October 5th: "In Countries like America, association between boys and girls starts at childhood, in kindergarten, and throughout school, and I don't think it is anything unusual."

In another section you wrote: "If you get invited, and it is all within the confines of being sociable, consult your American Mom. If a boy asks you to dance, I don't see any harm in that—but all these have to take place within the family or school environment."

Yet in another place you wrote: "You are a wise girl, but you lack experience."

What do you suggest I should do? If I don't participate in social activities, I will remain the same "wise and inexperienced girl." I don't understand why your letters are so contradictory. What annoys and surprises me is that you think the environment has changed me. Personally, I don't agree with the excess freedom of the American youth, and most teachers here agree with me too.

I just glanced at your October 5th letter again. This is what you say: "Learn to dance, it is an art. Participate in social gatherings and dance with your classmates, but at all times remember God."

Even to this day I'm baffled! Why did he bring God into our discussion?

In your October 27 letter you wrote: "...but stay away from dancing with them." Don't know which of your statements I'm to follow. I didn't know my simple question: "to attend or not to attend school dances" has taken so much of your time! All I wanted to know was whether you guys had any objections to my attending dances. You had discussed such deep, philosophical ideas, human behavioral sciences that had absolutely nothing to do with my question.

Okay, here is another question for you to answer. How do you propose I should gain experience without associating and having contact with others? When I return home, I will tell you what we thought of America and the Americans prior to this trip; similarities and differences.

In American Government class, we've been divided into two groups: the Federalists, and the Nationalists. I'm part of the Nationalist party. Just like regular political parties, students elect candidates to run for the city council, mayor, etc. All students then vote for the candidates. We learn how to vote. I'm a candidate for the Councilman position, and have to give a speech to the student body tomorrow. I'm not the only one, all the candidates have to make speeches.

Greetings to all, I have a ton of homework.

Love,

Manijeh

Sunday, November 5th, 1961

Hello Mom & Dad and sweet Sister,

Congratulations to Mother for the opening of her sewing classes.

Last Friday all the AFS students in this area went to northern Ohio for some sight-seeing. Each student spent the night with a different family in Rocky River (a town close to Avon Lake). I spent the night with a family who has two daughters and a son. In the evening there was a party just for the AFS students. American Red Cross volunteers were there to record our messages in our native tongue to send to our parents.

My American Dad is a candidate for the city of Avon Lake Councilman. His picture is in the paper and last night he gave a talk. Mrs. McClellan keeps asking me what to send you for Christmas. I said whatever she sends, you guys will like. Kathy just informed me that Christmas is on December 25th. So please send the Gaz and Pistachios right away, or early December. Christmas and New years are two different things. Christmas is the celebration of the birth of Christ, and January is the beginning of the New Year.

October 30th was the Halloween—similar to our "Charshanbe soori"—except that people wear funny costumes and mask. It is mostly for little kids who go from house to house and get candies

and cookies. But on October 28th, one of my school friends gave
a Halloween party. I dressed up as a doll with braded blonde hair,
and another girl dressed up as a male doll (Raggedy Ann and
Andy). We won a prize for best costumes and ate plenty of donuts
and drank lots of apple cider.

Last Sunday at church, Kathy and I attended the youth class and
talked about different religions. I shared information about my
religion and also learned a lot about theirs. Also, Kathy and I went
door to door to collect money for UNICEF. In our group, Kathy and I
collected the most.

As a 12th grader, I have to have senior picture taken. I went to the
photographer, and he took more than eight photos. It costs $30 but
the school is paying for my senior picture.

Mrs. Newman said there is a store here might be able to put a
heavy lining in my winter coat. We are not sure if that is possible.
A letter from AFS came and they said I could keep the check. I don't
need anything now, and don't have anything else to say.

Bye

Manijeh

Letter from Mrs. McClellan to my parents

November 5th, 1961

Dear Mrs. and Mr. Golbabai,

          I'm writing to you to tell you that Manijeh is in
very good health and seems to be very happy with us. Each

day sees her becoming more used to our way of living and
it seems to be easier for her.

There are, of course, some of our ways which
are very different for her to understand. I think her
biggest problem is "boys." The boy-girl relationship
seems to worry her very much. She read us your letter in
which you said that if you had not wanted her to do as we
do, you would not have let her come to the United States.
You are very wise and broad minded parents. However,
Manijeh feels that the only reason you said this is
because you knew she would not do it anyway. We feel that
Manijeh should not do anything that she feels is wrong.
She must live with herself, not only for the year that
she is here, but also for the many years of her life after
she leaves us. I'm only trying to tell you that we will
not push her into anything; that we think she is very
wise and knows best what is right for her. I hope that you
understand what I am trying to say.

Yesterday we had a meeting with parents of other
foreign exchange students. Several of the parents said
that their "daughters" wanted to date but couldn't get
dates with boys. And we said that our daughter, Manijeh,
didn't want to date but would have dates if she wanted
to. So you see, it just depends on what part of the world
the student comes from—what their attitude towards the
dating problem is.

I think Manijeh enjoyed her visit with the
other AFS students. They are a wonderful group of boys
and girls. It makes Lee and I feel very proud to be
privileged parents of Manijeh.

I hope Manijeh is no longer worried about being
warmly enough dressed for winter. I am sure that she has
warm enough clothes. We would not let her be improperly
dressed any more than we would our own children. Manijeh
is very concerned about clothes, cosmetics and perfume
as I understand all women in Iran are. She has very
lovely clothes and enough of them so do not worry about
that. With her lovely face and sparkling brown eyes, she
doesn't need beautiful clothes any way.

Lee is a candidate for the office of village
councilman. The election is Tuesday. Manijeh is a
candidate for the same office in the high school mock
election so she is receiving excellent first-hand
experience in our way of government.

If you feel that Manijeh has any problems, please
let me know. She always says that everything is fine.

Sincerely,

Kay and Lee McClellan

This letter of sixty-one years ago from my American mother
to my parents in Iran is significant and revealing to me. Not
only it gives me a glimpse into how I was perceived, but also
tells me the areas I had difficulty adjusting to: weather, food
and boys, all recurring themes. I chuckled at the impression I'd
given regarding Iranian women being concerned about "clothes,
cosmetics and perfumes." How did I do that? The part about
"clothes" I can understand because I was constantly worried
about the cold and I wanted to make sure I had enough warm
clothes for the winter. The "cosmetic" part baffles me, as I

had never used make-up before, not even a simple lipstick, in or outside of school. Maybe my interest in cosmetics peaked when I saw American girls wearing makeup to school, and I was paying attention, and wanted to learn more about cosmetics!

And the part about interest in "perfume" truly amused me. I recall my own mother in Iran always carried a tiny bottle of cologne or perfume in her purse. I did the same.

I remember before embarking on my journey to the U.S., Mother put a small bottle of 4711 (a German mild cologne) in my purse. The very first night the McClellan's picked me up at the Cleveland bus station, I sat up front between Mr. and Mrs. McClellan in their station wagon. Having been on the bus the entire day, I casually opened my purse, dabbed some cologne on myself to smell good. Soon after, I noticed tears running down my host father's eyes! It wasn't until much later that I learned he was allergic to perfume! At the time, I thought those were tears of joy for having me join their family!

November 7, 1961

Hello folks at home,

I'm writing this special letter to let you know my American Dad got elected as a Councilman. It is the first time he ran for office and won. Of the 2,000 people who voted, my Dad had 1,411 votes. There is a big celebration party going on downstairs in our house with lots of noise, laughter and food. It would be nice if you send him a congratulatory note. Similar election was held at school (mock election) for students to learn about government and I also got elected as a Councilman. It is 9:30 p.m. and I have not even started on my homework yet. Lots of friends are showing up, including Dr. and Mrs. Newman—he is our town doctor.

People here say a prayer before eating dinner. I've learned their prayer, and also have taught the family what we say: "In the name of God the merciful. God give us more blessings." Of course we all say it in Farsi. I took the English translation of Koran to church. I lack the knowledge of what is in Koran because we never had a Farsi translation, and I don't read Arabic!

We are getting a ton of phone calls tonight, and lots of action is going on downstairs. Bye!

November 10, 1961

Warm greetings to you all. Received three letters today.

Translated part of Uncle Jafar's letter for Mom McClellan. She was laughing so hard, and agreed Uncle is really funny!

The Forner's invited me over for Persian dinner. They had also invited two Iranian doctors who work at Cleveland hospitals. (**Dr Behzadi and Dr. Veladi)** I didn't like their attitude toward Iran. One of them, trying to be funny of course, was saying that he used to go to school on camel and if the camel was sick, he had to walk. Even as a joke, I didn't care for what he said. They were okay people. One was a former student of Uncle Jafar, and the other was from Tabriz.

By the way, my American family is adding a room to the house. I think a house should be built to be comfortable not to show off. When I return, I will work on that.

Why on earth would I say: "I will work on that?" I knew my father liked to buy and sell land; I guess that was his form of investing. I also knew he had a nice piece of property that Mother always said they would build on. But they never did, and eventually sold it. Maybe that is what I was thinking about, that if and when he wants to build, I will put in my own two-cents' worth into the plan!

By the way, I asked Mom McClellan about young men called "wolf." She laughed and said the term refers to men who blow whistles at girls in the streets, or make comments about their appearances! And I thought to myself, "Boy, you don't know about Tehran then, that at every step in the street we encounter wolves!" Please remember, Avon Lake is a very small town and most people know each other, especially everyone knows who I am.

Love,

Manijeh

November 16, 1961

Greetings Family Members,

Thanks for the photos. Kathy liked Jaleh's picture and said she is pretty.

Today Mom McClellan and I went shopping for your Christmas

gifts. She ordered a set of matching shirt and blouse for you. Here, sometimes husband and wife wear the same type and color shirt. She is also sending you some dried food items.

I'm so glad you recognize writing letters takes time. Not only I write to you, but also have to respond to my friends in America, AFS letters, etc. Very time-consuming.

Regarding financial matters: I now have $23 of my own money, and have not touched the $40 from Dr. Fayaz, but am keeping it.

I was at school till 6:30 p.m. yesterday working on the school newspaper—I was writing the headlines, not easy! For English class I'm supposed to write an essay on Islam and explain the religion. Mom McClellan doesn't want me to be doing homework all the time. She wants me to be more sociable and get together with friends and classmates. I reminded her that you have full confidence in her and whatever she thinks is best for me. I will do what Mom Mac thinks is best for me.

I like the shorthand class; we are all girls like my classes in Iran. We laugh a lot. The things I have observed here: people who are happy with good attitude are more liked. "Punctuality" and being on time is important, teachers are kind and friendly with the students. Stating the "truth" is another good characteristic in people here. They tell the truth even if it is not to their advantage!

The family is adding a room, and Dad McClellan is helping the carpenter and doing part of the work himself! Please make sure to write and congratulate him on winning the election.

I've learned quite a bit in these three months. There is so much fun in learning. Mom McClellan's sister has a sick child, therefore, we will not go to Michigan for Thanksgiving. My school principal had some kind of surgery. Mom and I went to pay him a visit, and he was appreciative. The family is doing well and everyone is busy with work and school.

Love,

Manijeh

November 25, 1961

Greetings to you all,

I wonder why Jaleh has not responded to her pen pal yet! It is impolite not to respond to a letter.

Last night Kathy and I, along with a group of young people from another church went to a movie in Cleveland and saw "King of Kings." It is the story of Christ—I can't explain it to you now. It was about Christ when he was born until the time they put him on a cross and killed him. I doubt if they would show this movie in Iran.

Mom McClellan just came back from Christmas shopping for you guys. She wants to send you boxes of cake mixes. They are in my room right now and I'm to translate the baking direction to Farsi. You said you want to send them some Persian tea. I think they will like that. At this time all the stores are decorated for Christmas with all kinds of colorful lights.

Uncle Jafar asked if there is a way I could stay in the U.S. for college. I don't know and that is not something I think about.

True, life's comfort, entertainment and activities are much more interesting here than in Iran, but I guess I prefer living in Iran.

Enclosed are a few photos of the homecoming king and queen —I gave them gifts from Iran. The celebration was in our school gymnasium and you can see the basketball hoop in the background. Also, you can see what the girls are wearing to the homecoming, which is not as big an event as the Prom for seniors. I think I will need a prom dress.

Love to all, Manijeh

A newspaper article appeared as soon as I arrived in Avon Lake. The caption said: Taste of American Food. In this photo I'm surrounded by the McClellan family.

My family often enjoyed eating in the backyard, picnic style.

Dr. & Mrs. Newman & family. I'm (left) sitting next to Mrs. Newman, who was the AFS liaison.

Jane and I enjoyed playing with "Lady," the family dog, a gentle Collie.

Above: Visiting the County Fair with Aunt Gloria (left), and my host parents. As a city girl, I was fascinated by the huge farm animals.

Below: Mr. J.I King, Superintendent of the Avon Lake Schools. He wanted me to attend college in the U.S.

Right: Mrs. Bomberger, the wife of U.S. agricultural advisor in Iran. She was my informal tutor and an English conversation partner.

Below: A photo with my siblings. Left to right: Tom, Manijeh, Jane and Ted.

6 The Journal, Lorain, Ohio Wednesday, January 10, 1962

First Engagement

Exchange Student Speaks To Women At Avon Lake

AVON LAKE — The first public speaking engagement of Miss Manigeh Golbabai, Avon Lake's foreign exchange student, was at Monday's meeting of the Women's Association of the Avon Lake United Presbyterian C h u r c h, which she attends while here with her American parents, Mr. and Mrs. M. Lee McClellan, 33215 Lake Rd. She was introduced by Mrs. McClellan.

She showed color slides of her country and its customs, told about her family and her own life and the dating and marriage routine followed there. Appearing in an ancient, tribal costume, she stated the dress of today is modern and along Parisian fashion.

Arriving in this country in August of 1961, Manigeh is attending Avon Lake High School, and will remain here until June, when she will join other American Field Service students for a one-month tour of the eastern states and Washington, D. C.

Mrs. Alan Moir, association president, presided. Refreshments were served by Mrs. Richard Leppert and members of Dorcas Circle.

Mrs. Moir, Left, And Miss Golbabai

Start of my speaking engagements. Wearing a costume for the first time felt funny and uncomfortable.

Wearing my saddle shoes and bobby socks, most popular at the time!

Top Inset: My senior picture in the yearbook, The Shore Log 1962. Below the photo my school activities were listed: Language Club, Student Council, Girls' Glee, Spectrum (school yearbook), Class Officer, Student Librarian, Pep Club, G.A.A., Nemerohs, Girls' Ensemble.

Bottom Inset: After I married my husband, I modeled a borrowed Kurdish costume—his family is originally Kurdish.

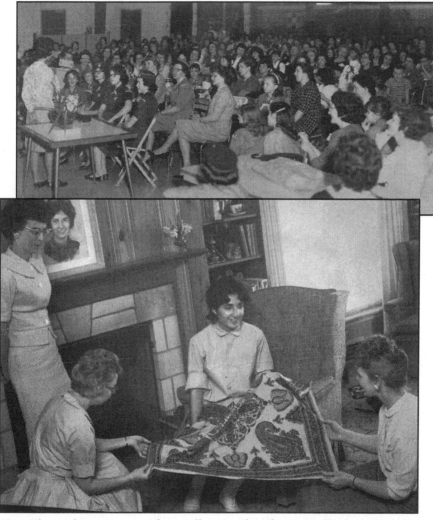

*Top: The audience at one of my talks in a church. I usually showed slides
and answered questions. I'm standing with my back to the camera.*

*Bottom: Showing and telling about Iranian handicraft. The framed
picture on the mantelpiece is a painting of my senior photo, a gift from
an art student from Avon Lake High School.*

Dad McClellan invited me to the Annual Father, Son, and Daughter Night of the Lorain Works Management Club. Two other AFS students also attended. Left to right: Dad, me, Eckart Winterhoff (West Germany) and Fauzia Rafique (Pakistan)

Many families in the community invited me to have dinner with them and their children to learn about Iran.

I'm with Judy Fischer, one of my high school friends. Judy's younger sister was my sister, Jaleh's, pen pal for a while.

Iranian Girl Will Be Avon Club Speaker

AVON—Miss Manigeh Golbabai of Teheran, Iran, will be the guest speaker when the Avon Welcome Wagon Newcomers Club meets Monday at 8:15 p.m. in the community room of the Central Bank.

Miss Golbabai will speak of her life in Iran. She is a student at Avon Lake High School.

Plans for the month of January were made by the executive board of the club at a meeting held this week at the home of Mrs. Lawrence Davee.

Mrs. Gary Newman was appointed chairman of arrangements for the annual sponsors' dinner, scheduled to be held by the group in February.

Hostesses for Monday night's meeting will be Mrs. Curtiss Radcliffe, Mrs. Charles Brewer and Mrs. John Crober

6 The Journal, Lorain, Ohio
Wednesday, March 7, 1962

Exchange Students On Panel

AMHERST — Eckart Winterhoss, Hanover, Germany, exchange student to Vermilion High School, Manigh Golbabbai, Tehran, Iran, exchange student to Avon Lake High School, and Alicia Mora of La Jose, Costa Rica, attending Steele High School, served on a panel and discussed their countries at the meeting of the Junior-Senior PTA held at Steele High School.

Leonard Lyle was moderator of the panel, and the students told about customs, schools, teen-agers and their families in their native countries.

Mrs. Richard Thutt, vice president, was in charge of the business meeting. Mrs. William Wheatley gave the invocation.

Announcement was made of the North Central Conference of PTA's to be held at Elyria High School April 11. Registration will take place at 12:30

I gave over 30 talks to various organizations, and always there was a write up about it in the paper

*Right: Sitting on the lap
of a young man who
called himself "Santa"
felt very strange!*

*Below: The McClellan's
Christmas card—
December 1961.*

Top: Visiting Mrs. Newman and her family, Christmas 1961.

Right: I grew wheat (Sabzeh) the Iranian way to celebrate the Persian New Year (Norouz).

Top Left: Me and Janet Newman at the Prom (photo courtesy of Janet—I didn't have any prom photos)

Top Right: I'm (left) with Kathy (right) at the Prom. My mother made me the Prom dress and mailed it to Avon Lake.

Bottom Left: Doctor and Mrs. Newman with their daughter, Janet, at the Prom.

Bottom Right: This is the only photo of me and my date to the Prom— Jane was trying to hug me.

Top: Receiving my High School Diploma.

Bottom: The 1962 graduating class of Avon Lake High School.

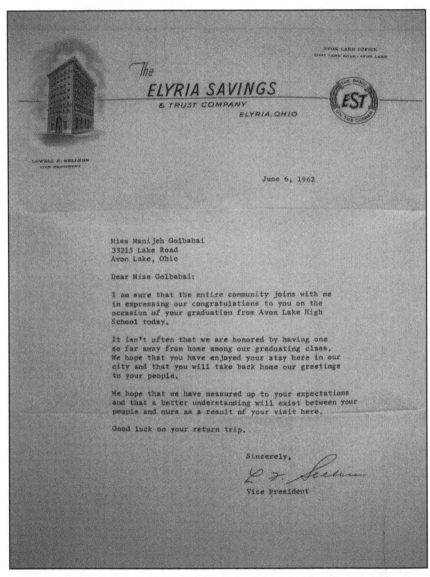

The ELYRIA SAVINGS
& TRUST COMPANY
ELYRIA, OHIO

AVON LAKE OFFICE

LOWELL F. SELLERS
VICE PRESIDENT

June 6, 1962

Miss Manijeh Golbabai
33215 Lake Road
Avon Lake, Ohio

Dear Miss Golbabai:

I am sure that the entire community joins with me
in expressing our congratulations to you on the
occasion of your graduation from Avon Lake High
School today.

It isn't often that we are honored by having one
so far away from home among our graduating class.
We hope that you have enjoyed your stay here in our
city and that you will take back home our greetings
to your people.

We hope that we have measured up to your expectations
and that a better understanding will exist between your
people and ours as a result of your visit here.

Good luck on your return trip.

Sincerely,

Vice President

A nice congratulatory letter from the VP of the local bank, Mr. Sellers.

Farewell Dinner Given For Pupil

AVON LAKE — A farewell dinner was given at the M. Lee McClellan home, 33215 Lake Rd., Wednesday by Manijeh Golbabai, foreign exchange student from Tehran, Iran, for native friends whom she met while here.

The McClellans have been Manijeh's American parents for nearly the past year.

The main course of the meal was prepared by Manijeh in Iranian style, and consisted of round steak "shiskebobs" made of cubes of the meat marinated in onion juice, and cooked over an open fire outdoors, and rice as only her people cook it. Using a small amount of water, and left unstirred during the cooking process, the lid is weighted down so as to retain the steam, the bottom of the content of the kettle forming a delicately browned crust.

Enthusiastic over the food as prepared in their homeland were Dr. Najad Behzadi, anesthetist at Fairview Park Hospital, Fairview Park, and Mrs. Behzadi; Dr. Manochehr Aboozia, surgeon at Lutheran Hospital, Cleveland, and Mrs. Aboozia; Dr. Habid Zeladi, chief obstetrician at Fairview Park.

Present also were Rev. and Mrs. George Forner of Bay Presbyterian Church, who spent two years in Tehran prior to coming to Bay Village, and who, in many instances, were interpreters as it were, for the McClellans. Guests from here were Mrs. William Davis and Mrs. John Newman, in addition to Mr. and Mrs. McClellan and family.

Busy at present packing for the first step in her homeward journey, Manijeh will leave here Saturday for Cleveland where she will spend several days. A bus will then pick up all the foreign exchange students meeting in Cleveland and leave for a tour of the New England states before embarking for home.

Before I left Avon Lake, a few Iranian doctors in the Cleveland area came over for a Persian dinner of rice and Kabob.

After a year in the U.S. my family thought I looked like an American girl!

A Farewell Dinner. Mom and Dad McClelland are standing behind me.

A Farewell Dinner

A farewell dinner was given at the home of Mr. and Mrs. M. Lee McClellan by Manijeh Golbabai, foreign exchange student from Tehran, Iran, for native friends whom she met while here.

Enthusiastic over the food as prepared in their homeland

were Dr. and Mrs. Manoocheher Aboozia, from Lutheran Hospital, Dr. and Mrs. Nejad Behzadi from Fairview Park Hospital, Dr. Habib Velzdi from Fairview Park Hospital, Rev. and Mrs. Geo. Forner of Bay Presbyterian Church,

Newman.

Manijeh left Saturday for Cleveland where she will spend several days. A bus will then pick up all the foreign exchange students meeting in Cleveland and leave for a tour of the New England states before embarking for home.

Top: *At the end of our bus tour, 2222 students from all over the world gathered in Washington D.C. The event was known as Midway. Here I am with the Iranian students, gathered under the Iranian flag. I'm standing 3rd from left.*

Bottom: *Congressman Moser of Ohio gave me and three other AFS students a personal tour of the Capitol building. From left: me, Eckart (Germany), Fauzia (Pakistan), Congressman Moser, and Solveig (Norway).*

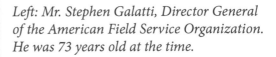

Left: Mr. Stephen Galatti, Director General of the American Field Service Organization. He was 73 years old at the time.

Middle: On board of the Seven Seas, a plain no frill ship which transported AFS students to Europe. We ate our meals at long tables, and they gave us funny hats to wear (I don't remember the occasion!)

I visited Mom and Dad McClellan on numerous occasions since my return in 1968. Here I am with my husband and son on a visit to Avon Lake.

Top: *I was matron of honor at Kathy's wedding. L to R Jane, Kathy, me.*

Bottom: *In 2015 Mom was in memory care and did not remember me, but said my voice sounded familiar. She passed away in 2016 at the age of 93.*

Top: We celebrated Mom McClellan's 92nd birthday in 2015. Standing: from left: me, Jane and Kathy. Sitting: Mom and Ted.

Bottom: In 2015, while visiting Avon Lake, I spent one afternoon talking and reminiscing with Mr. Turner who had helped me with my studies in 1961. Sadly, he passed away in 2017 – he was 85 years old.

Left: In 1983 I became a host mother to an AFS student from Argentina, Juan Jose Cruces. My husband (Khosrow) and I with our two boys— Juan (left) and Kas (right).

Below: In 2022 Juan visited us while in the US. Same L-R. We were so happy to see him we recreated the same photo 39 years later.

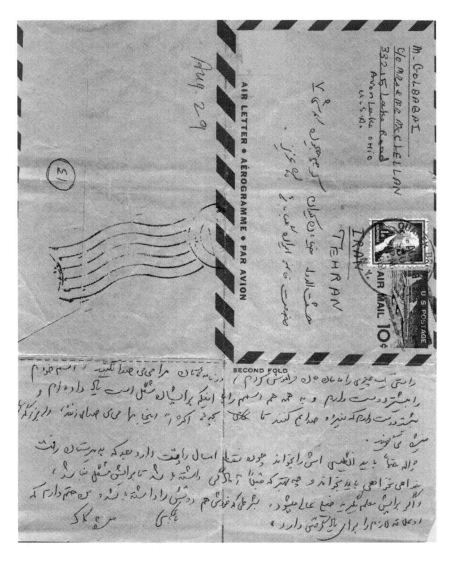

An Aerogram to my family in Tehran, August 29, 1961. My father numbered it as the 13th piece of mail they had received from me. Written in Farsi, the US Post Office needed the country and city in English and the Iranian post office needed the address in Farsi. Even with the language difference, both post offices always came through.

Chapter Five

Monday, December 4th

Dear Father,

Happy Birthday to Jaleh. She will be going to secondary school next year. Hope she likes the watch you got her for her birthday.

My American parents and I went to a special gathering /meeting of all the AFS volunteers held in Cleveland. Mr. Galatti, the director general of AFS gave a talk. After the meeting, I spoke with him and learned that they plan to send American students to Iran in the near future. Of course it will be only for a summer exchange program. Tell Jaleh to work hard on her English, so maybe in the future we can host an American student.

I went to church with my family on Sunday, and then we attended a concert in Cleveland and listened to Christmas songs, all related to the birth of Jesus Christ.

Okay father, I have a question, related to the same question Uncle Jafar asked me in his letter. Do you think there is a way I can stay here and go to college? There are five universities in Ohio. One is in Columbus and the other four are around the state. I'm not sure if I can stay beyond the one year. Could you research and find out if it is possible.

This morning Mom McClellan picked me up from school around 11:00 a.m. and we went to a meeting where Congressman Moser of Ohio spoke to a group of ladies. The ladies asked him all kinds of questions about the government, policies, etc. and he answered them all. Afterward, I met him. American women are well-informed and participate in politics and elections.

At the end of my AFS year, I spent a few days in Washington D.C. and Congressman Moser gave me and three other foreign students a tour of the Capitol Building, and we had our pictures taken on the steps of the Capitol.

I'm finding out that American youth have responsibilities commensurate with their freedom. Most of my classmates have jobs, and it is not because their parents are poor and they need the money. When I compare them to some lazy Iranian kids who even demand a glass of water to be handed to them, I wonder and scratch my head!

Oh, My! I'm paying attention to the real American life, and probably am discarding the images about America, based on the movies one sees! Real understanding of real people is taking shape. I'm observing the differences and similarities between the two cultures: family life, work, responsibilities, and participation in the political process. The purpose of this whole AFS experience was understanding between nations, and I guess it was sinking in.

I had a cute and interesting letter from Mrs. Bomberger. She wrote, "Talk to all your male friends, and think of them as if they are Mr. Sholevar."

Javad Sholevar was a relative of my father. He had finished medical school in Iran and was doing his residency in Pennsylvania. He also knew Mr. & Mrs. Bomberger, and I'm assuming he was an official translator for Mr. Bomberger at the Ministry of Agriculture, but I am not certain.

Cleveland was spectacular and all the stores were decorated for Christmas. I'm well and healthy.

Love,

Manijeh

Letter from AFS staff to my parents in Iran

American Field Service .
International Scholarships
313 East 43rd Street
New York 17, N.Y.

December 4, 1961

Mr. & Mrs. Hassan Golbabai

7 Keyvan St.

Hishmatdouleh Ave.

Tehran, Iran

Dear Mr. & Mrs. Golbabai:

This past Saturday night when I was at an AFS conference
in Cleveland, Ohio I had the great pleasure of seeing
Manijeh, who came with Mr. & Mrs. McClellan to hear Mr.
Galatti speak. I had met Manijeh last summer when she
first arrived here from Iran and have been writing to
her ever since.

Manijeh looked so pretty and well. She smiled
continually and assured me that she was very happy with
the McClellan family.

I was very sorry that we didn't have more time to talk
together, and I am looking forward to next summer when I
shall have a chance to see her again.

Sincerely,

Joan Patt (Miss)

AFS Staff

**My American Mom, Mrs. McClellan, sent my parents another
letter. Needless to say, my father had kept that one too!**

December 8, 1961

Dear Mr. and Mrs. Golbabai,

Your very nice letter arrived here today—also yesterday
all of the packages that you sent to us arrived. I did
not tell Manijeh that they came. I will keep them for a

surprise for all of the children on Christmas morning.

I asked Manijeh to explain to you that the gift we have ordered for Kamron has not yet come. We do not want to mail any of the gifts until we can mail them all. Since you do not celebrate Christmas, I hope their being late will not matter to you.

We have had a very mild winter this year. Today we had our first snow fall and then not much of that. I think that Manijeh is warm enough and she seems to be looking forward to the winter now.

Our busy life becomes even more busier as the Christmas season approaches. This is the season for cleaning and decorating the house, for new clothes, shopping for gifts, sending Christmas cards, parties and increased church activities. Manijeh is looking forward to all of this. The streets are decorated, the stores and homes also. Between Christmas and New Year, the children do not attend school. They visit each other, have parties, go coasting and ice skating.

The postman who delivered your packages to me was very interested in the fact that the packages said "New Year's Gift" instead of Christmas gift. So I explained your religion to him as best I could. He stayed for about 20 minutes while I told him all about Islam, Iran and your customs. Today the city building inspector came to check the electrical wiring in our new room. He also wanted to know all about Manijeh, her religion and her customs. So you see, in many different ways people are becoming acquainted with Iran and the differences and the similarities of our culture.

The children and I all went Christmas shopping last
night. I think Manijeh enjoyed it because there are so
many lovely things to see.

We certainly do wish that you could be here at this
time of year. I'm sure that we would enjoy each other's
company even though we could not converse freely. From
things that Manijeh and I discuss, I'm sure that we
think and believe alike on many subjects.

    Very truly yours,

    Kay McClellan

I'm not sure if even today the ordinary Iranians differentiate
between Christmas and the New Year. In Iran, Persian New
Year (Norouz) is a big national holiday. Schools are closed
for a couple of weeks. Wearing new clothes, exchanging gifts,
visiting and partying, are all part of the celebration, which is
similar to Christmas in America. But Norouz is not a religious
holiday, it is the arrival of Spring and the beginning of a new
year that is being celebrated. It would be more logical to equate
the birth of Christ to the birth of Prophet Mohammad in Islam.
However, sixty years ago, the Christian community in Tehran
(The Armenians) celebrated the arrival of the western calendar
with parties, hats, gift-giving, etc. Even today, I hear from
family members in Iran who send their greetings in January for
the celebration of western New Year!

December 10, 1961

Dear Mom and Dad,

Last night I had a dream about all of you. I was dreaming that I came back to Iran, but all my clothes and belongings were left in the U.S. Actually, I had a similar dream a few nights ago, that I had returned but left my suitcases in the U.S.!

It snowed here yesterday, but not very much, there will be more soon! A classmate of mine was going to visit Wooster College. Her parents asked me to join them. It took one and a half hours to get to Wooster College. We visited the library, chemistry lab, music department, girls' dorm, cafeteria, bathrooms and laundry room. It was a beautiful college. American colleges are a lot different from American high schools.

I think my classmate, Cheryl, was making a college visit at the time. I was so glad they asked me to go along.

Last night my host parents went to a dance. I fixed up Mom McClellan's hair and she looked really nice.

A group of ladies who are members of the AFS chapter here in Avon Lake invited me to dinner. They asked all kinds of questions, and answering some of them required knowledge and skill. Some questions were really hard to answer. For example, one lady asked, "Is it true that the new administration doesn't allow people to spend their money outside of Iran?"

I said "Yes." She asked, "Then why did Queen Farah spend $2,400 in Paris buying jewelry?"

Instances like these, I have no answer and don't know what to say.

All I could think of was to smile and remind them that the Queen is young and very nice, or she probably was spending her own money! Or they would ask, "When did the country's name change from Persia to Iran?" Reading the books you sent me made it easier to answer these types of questions. I think my knowledge about Iran has increased now that I'm away from it. I'm thinking and researching subjects that I never thought about while I was in Iran.

The turkey dinner I mentioned earlier was neither for Christmas, nor Easter. It was for "Thanksgiving."

Tomorrow, all of us who have been elected **(I was elected as a councilman)** are going to the municipal building to visit and run the city for one day.

We had a pep rally for the basketball players to encourage all the students to rally around the team and go to the game. Mr. Turner, who teaches foreign languages, and I were on the stage and spoke in different languages to motivate the student body. Mr. Turner spoke in Russian, Spanish, Latin and French. Yours truly spoke in Farsi, Arabic and Turkish. As you know, I don't know Arabic. So all I did was recite the prayer in Arabic which had nothing to do with basketball and the game! And thanks to Naneh, the Turkish maid, I remembered a few practical words to utter in Turkish language.

Nothing else to write about. I'm really well, and please, Mother, don't repeat your question again!

Love,

Manijeh

December 17, 1961

Greetings to all.

Jaleh's excellent letter to her pen pal arrived. She has beautiful handwriting. There is another 6th grader here who wants to be pen pal with Jaleh. Let me know if you want to correspond with her and I will give her your address.

Everyone is busy here preparing for Christmas. Most homes are decorated with lights, and Mom McClellan goes shopping everyday! So many interesting things to see that I sometimes wish I had two sets of eyes. The family's Christmas card photo turned out well. Mom will send you one.

Our Christmas vacation starts December 21st and we will go back on January 3rd. I've developed an ingrown toe nail which has become infected. The minute I said my toe hurts, Mom took me to Dr. Newman.

Wish you could be here—the house is decorated with Christmas stuff, statue of Santa Claus, candles, greens, etc. On Sunday, only Mom and I went to church—Kathy slept in and Dad had work to do. This week before Christmas the church was also exciting, all decorated and all singing. This evening Kathy and I and another classmate went caroling. We sang to old and sick people. This was also organized through our church.

It might have been a nursing home we visited.

Grandpa and Grandma are coming from Michigan to spend Christmas with us. I do have enough Christmas gifts for the family —have kept them as a surprise. As an elected councilman I visited the municipal building, power plant, water works, etc. Afterwards, the group was invited to dinner at a nice restaurant in Avon Lake. We don't have a Christmas tree at home yet, but school has one, and I helped decorate it. If I'm late in sending letters, don't worry. It is Christmas time, and just like our own Norouz, there is a lot of work and activity going on.

The new room addition is about to finish. Dad McClellan is an electrical engineer and is doing all the electrical work himself. He even fixes the washer and dryer by himself. As I write these, Kathy is babysitting, my brothers are sleep, and Dad is working downstairs in the new room. Mom just finished doing the laundry and is ironing. In short, everyone works here and they all get the work done cheerfully. Last night I babysat for a family and they have a color T.V. That was my first time to watch a color T.V.

Love to all,

Manijeh

December 20, 1961

Today after lunch Mrs. Newman picked me up from school to go shopping. She bought me a white wool dress as Christmas gift. We then had afternoon tea together in a restaurant. She is such a kind and intelligent woman. Told me she has written to you, and that she does not expect a response, as it is her responsibility to write and let you know how I'm doing.

Tonight after dinner we all went and bought a big beautiful Christmas tree, which we will decorate on Sunday. The kids are very excited, me too as it is my first Christmas, and most interesting. Mrs. Bomberger wrote and explained Christmas to me, and what it means. Please expect the letters take longer to reach you—post office is very busy these days.

For my English class, I must read a book and give a summary report. I chose a book from the school library, *Persia is My Heart,* by Najmeh Najafi, written in 1953. I've not finished reading it, but you can imagine how much the country has changed since 10 years ago. Something to talk about!

Regarding my financial situation: received a $14 check from AFS, added to my $19, now I have a total of $33. I still have not cashed Dr. Fayaz's check.

Nothing more to report. Good night.

Manijeh

December 27, 1961

Dear Mother and Father,

Hope you are both well, I do miss you. Okay, let's talk about Christmas and the gifts.

On December 25th we all got up early, and still in our pajamas, started coming down the stairs while Dad McClellan rolled the camera. His parents came from Michigan two days before Christmas. We all sat on the floor. Lots of wrapped presents were under the tree. Dad distributed the boxes, one at a time—names were written on the boxes. I received fourteen gifts (counted them all). One of the boys in my class gave me a necklace.

Mrs. Newman also thanks you a lot for sending her the pistachios. I gave her a cigarette holder, and a bracelet to her daughter. Aunt Gloria and her husband showed up and took a lot of pictures.

By the way Mother, you said you want to make me a formal gown. Thank you, this is wonderful. The formals here are not only expensive around $30, but also they all look alike.

If you look at the *Etelaat'e Banovan*, magazine #234, on page 13, there is a photo of a formal gown which is suitable for prom. I would like it in white, floor length. Please give me your opinion on that dress. We do have time, prom is in spring.

Love,

Manijeh

Chapter Six

January 2, 1962

Dear Mother and Father,

This is my last day of vacation. Starting January 5th, I will begin giving talks. Last night one of my teachers who will accompany me on these speeches, Mr. and Mrs. Forner (as you know they spent two years in Iran), and I got together and went through my slides. I have 66 slides only 43 could be used. I don't have slides of Persepolis or historical places in Iran. The Forners had taken some good photos and I'll be using some of their slides.

We had an interesting guest also. He is an Iranian doctor by the name of Manoochehr Aboozia, has been here four years and works at a hospital in Cleveland. He arrived around 2:00 p.m. and stayed for dinner. Aunt Gloria and her husband also were present and along with Mom and Dad McClellan, they asked him all kinds of political questions, especially about the elections in Iran. He said, "In Iran people do vote, but then someone else's name comes out of the ballot box!" You can imagine how surprised these folks were. Mom

McClellan with wide eyes asked him how is such a thing possible? He responded, "People have no control over the elections." He also asked the McClellans, "Why is America sending funds to Iran? The funds do not get used properly and only a few people pocket the money." Or he said, "Bribery in Iran is very common. When someone does anything wrong, all he has to do is pay a bribe and will be freed."

I was sad, and I felt his words were humiliating Iran as a country, and did not participate in their discussion. I guess I don't have the experience or the expertise to talk politics here, and don't engage in political discussions. All I could do was to show him the airmail newspapers I receive and let him know that he has been out of Iran four years and that improvements and progress are being made.

Regarding my upcoming talks, I wish I had slides from our own family. I have the photos, but slides would have been good from our family or even mother's sewing class with her students. Tonight I made Kotlet for dinner. It did not look good, but tasted okay and the family liked it—at least they said so. Maybe they were being polite!

A letter from AFS arrived telling me that I will leave here June 27th and apparently will have a three-week bus tour of the eastern part of the U.S.

Love, Manijeh

January 3rd, 1962

Dear Father,

I received your letter of December 24 along with letters from two friends. Usually, I read your letter last so that I take my time and ponder on your words. You asked about the gifts you sent to the McClellans. Yes, the nuts and candies and the inlaid boxes and the jewelry were all wonderful. They opened them carefully, and now they are on display for friends who come to visit. I thank you and Uncle Jafar for all these gifts, but please do not send any more gifts.

Today I received my 5th monthly check from AFS which indicates I have been in the U.S. five months—seven more to go. You asked me what I have learned within this time period, and how I have benefitted by associating with the American youth. So I'm responding to you right away.

Please note that I do not change myself in order to follow others. Apparently this is the characteristic others have also noticed about me: Mrs. Newman, the McClellan's, and the teachers at school. As Mom McClellan has written you, they let me to be free to choose what is right for me. There are behaviors and way of life that are considered normal and acceptable here. But as an Iranian girl, I know they are not accepted in the Iranian society. Therefore, I do not imitate or follow what I think is not appropriate for me. What do you think I do in such instances? Close my eyes? No, absolutely not. I open my eyes even wider in order to see and understand more and learn the truth about the American way of life. There are AFS students who are crazy about the lifestyle here and want to follow everything without analyzing. To these people I would say not to forget some of the nice values from our own country. This year, of which five months have already passed, will be a valuable experience in my life. I have carefully been observing others, and gaining experience without being part of the experiment. This is what you have taught me: by learning from other people's experiences, we can save time and gain the necessary information for our own success. I'm 12,000 miles away, but your words of advice ring in my head.

I feel comfortable in my surroundings here and have explained to others the expectations in the Iranian society.

Enclosed with the monthly check from AFS was a letter from Mr. Galatti. He asked all AFS students to read a book called *In This Year* and then give him our input. Between reading this book, my homework, preparing for my speeches, I really don't have any free time. Most nights I go to bed after midnight. Mom McClellan insists I go to bed earlier and says rest and getting enough sleep is important.

My father had mailed me a bunch of books and wanted me to read them. Somehow I had to let him know that I did not have time for his reading assignments.

I will leave Avon Lake June 27th and will have a three-week tour of the eastern United States. In August our lives will be back to normal.

Your daughter,

Manijeh

Mrs. John W. Newman

33880 Lake Road

Avon Lake, Ohio

January 4, 1962

Dear Mr. & Mrs. Golbabai,

How very kind it was of you to send me the New Years
presents of candy and nuts. We have all enjoyed them
very much, especially my father who is visiting us for
the holidays. He wishes that we could get your delicious
salt-flavored nuts in the stores here. Please accept
our thanks.

It was a pleasure to receive your letter; soon I will be
writing to you again about Manijeh

Yours Sincerely,

Dr. & Mrs. Newman

January 8, 1962

Hi Everyone,

Mother asked me about the formal dress she is going to make me.
Every occasion here requires certain type of clothing. They won't
wear party clothes to school, shorts are for picnics and outings,
and formal settings require long gowns. The photo in the magazine
I mentioned is appropriate for Prom. Please make it long with
puffy skirt. The bodice is lacey fabric and the skirt is satin. The
flower attached to the bodice is also white. Formal dresses cost
somewhere around $30 to $90. If you make it for me, not only it

will cost less, but also it would be unique and nobody will have a dress like it.

I bought myself a pair of long pants. The ones you sent and the one I brought with me are too tight. Maybe they shrunk! (**I fail to mention that maybe I have gained weight!**)

Salted pistachios are very popular here. Aunt Gloria asked if she could send you money to have you send her the nuts. I told her I didn't know. I went to a basketball game in a nearby town with two other AFS students, Fauzia from Pakistan and Eckart from Germany. The three of us are good friends.

I must hurry to have dinner and go to my speaking engagement. Mother, don't forget the dress. It has to have puffy skirt and must get here by March, otherwise I will not be able to use it.

Writing later: it is 11:30 p.m. now. My talk went well, and now Mom McClellan is telling Dad how well I did. I wore the costume you sent. The ladies were all from our church and asked a lot of questions. My humorous jokes added to the talk and they laughed a lot. They wanted to know how I was selected for this scholarship, wanted to know about schools and life of women in Iran. They said I spoke English well, and that pleased Mom McClellan.

I've talked too much today, better stop writing. Don't forget about the formal dress.

Love,

Manijeh

January 13, 1962

Hello Folks,

Miss you all, especially Jaleh, Mehran and Kamran. Kathy
is babysitting, Mom and Dad are at a party; my brothers are
downstairs watching T.V. and I just told them to quit and go to bed.

It was nice that Mother wrote to Kathy by referring to her, "My
dear daughter, Kathy," but why did she sign as "Mrs. Golbabai,"
rather than "your mother." People here are aware that Mother
doesn't know English, and most probably the secretary in father's
office has translated it into English. But please don't be formal and
don't use complicated literary words. Simple words will do.

The McClellan children are writing you "Thank You" notes for the
gifts you sent. This is a custom here that when one receives a gift
or is invited to dinner, one must quickly send a "Thank You" note. I
do so using AFS stationary.

I have 70 good slides to show during my talks. Mrs. Newman brought
over photos she took of me before Christmas at her house. Today, I
read a whole bunch on Iranian history, to increase my knowledge
about my own country. It is funny, when it is not school requirement,
one learns history and geography quickly because one needs to know!

As I mentioned before, my family has two cars: a Chevrolet which
is big and new, and an old Plymouth. This afternoon Mom and Dad
McClellan bought a new Plymouth which Dad takes to work.

Please tell Jaleh not to get upset if her grades are not high. Grades
are not important, only the knowledge one gains is. Look, I got
high marks in history and geography, but they were of no use to
me. Now I have to really read and study those subjects to be able

to give talks and answer questions about Iran. I'm gaining a lot of experience, which I will share when I get back.

Love,

Manijeh

January 22, 1962

Hello there,

It is no exaggeration that I have no time to scratch my head! Final exams, attending gatherings, and giving talks, have consumed all my time. I went ice-skating on Lake Erie. It was wonderful to walk on the Lake which is frozen all the way to Canada. As far as my eyes could see, there was ice and snow—a magnificent view.

What a change in attitude! I'm not complaining about cold and snow any more!

On the 12th day of Christmas, they throw away the Christmas tree. First people bring their trees to a specific location and a machine collects them all. It is called "tree burning" ceremony. The mayor of Avon Lake spoke, the school choir sang (I was among them) and the weather was very cold, so we all had long pants and boots on.

Second semester has started and in place of speech, I'm taking American History. Now that my English has improved, I'm learning both American Government and American History.

Thank you, father, the books you sent have arrived. When I mentioned to Mom McClellan about the contents of the books, she said she is sorry they are not in English. I gave a talk to a woman's organization in a nearby town. One woman asked my age and then said she is surprised at my self-confidence. I spoke calmly and interjected humor. All is going well with the family, I'm having fun and feel comfortable.

Tonight is Parent Teacher Conferences. Parents visit the school and sit in their children's classroom. Some students are guides—I am one of the guides.

Mother, don't forget about the Prom dress. It has to be floor length, I will wear it with high heels.

Love,

Manijeh

My goodness, I'm really making a pest of myself by reminding Mother in every letter about the prom dress, color, fluffy skirt, etc. What I did not write them, however, was the fact that I had been asked to the prom by several classmates. I accepted the invitation of one individual who kept asking me on a daily basis, and I finally agreed. He was the son of our city judge, and the family was a friend of the McClellan's. Everyone knew Judge Jenson and I went to Prom with his son.

January 24, 1962

Dear Baba Jaan,

Today at lunch, Mr. King, the Superintendent of the Avon Lake Schools, came to the cafeteria and asked me to go visit him in his office. He is a serious old gentleman and the students respect him a lot. He also appears to be a wise and kind man. In his office, he asked me about my studies, and what I plan to do when I get back and which college I will attend. I told him I'm thinking of medical school and that I ranked third in all my science classes. We talked about Iranian universities. He then asked me if I wanted to continue my education in the U.S. I said I would, if the conditions were right. He said I could study medicine here, and then asked if I was interested in any other field besides medicine. I said I would be interested in a Ph.D. in English literature, or psychology or education and that I wouldn't mind studying in these field. The only problem was the cost of college education.

We talked about different colleges and he mentioned the name of a college, the name of which escapes me now, but said it is near Mississippi, good climate, small college and offers scholarship to foreign students. The president of the college is a friend of Mr. King. He said he would write a letter to that school and inquire about scholarships.

These folks are extremely happy with my hard work and disciplined behavior. In order to get an American Diploma in Ohio, one must study both American Government and American History, both of which I'm taking right now. Therefore, I will officially be a graduate of an American high school.

What are your thoughts on the subject, now that our Superintendent of school is ready to help me get into a college? Your opinion and consent is important. I told Mr. King I would have to consult my father and will let him know. Please give me your thoughts. I think it is an excellent opportunity.

Mr. King and I talked a lot. He likes that I respect others, and the way I talk to people. He agreed that I would need financial aid the first two years. I'm asking for your guidance,

Regards to all, with love,

Manijeh

Chapter Seven

February 3, 1962

Hello Dear Folks at Home,

Your beautiful photos arrived. Mom and Aunt Mehri look beautiful, and their hair style is the latest fashion which is now beginning to become popular here. Photos from Mother, Father and dear Jaleh are priceless. Mom McClellan said Jaleh is a "Glamour" girl. Look up the word in the dictionary. Hollywood might offer Uncle Jafar a role!

The Forners invited me over the weekend. Apparently two Iranian doctors live in their vicinity. They invited one of them for Persian dinner of Chelo Kabob, yogurt and cucumber. Two skewers of kabob were left over, and they gave it to the dog!

It is the fourth time that our school basketball team has lost. We were all upset but couldn't do anything about it. After the game, Kathy and I and a bunch of friends went to Acquamarine (a restaurant) and got something to eat—I had a big bowl of strawberry ice cream.

The airmail subscription of the daily paper arrives regularly and keeps me informed of what is happening in Iran. However, before I learned of the riots at the University, the newspapers here had reported it.

Perhaps that is why Mr. King wanted to discuss my college plans. He knew about the riots at the University of Tehran.

Mrs. Bomberger wrote me from Philippines and said she thought of Mother because they have beautiful fabrics there. She wants to send you, via me, some wool fabric. She also said, "You probably are going to write this to your mother right away, and she will quickly reciprocate by sending me a gift." She seriously asked me not to tell you about her gift. You see, I didn't! Actually, Americans do not give gifts in order to get something in return. Mom McClellan explained to me that they give gifts in order to make the other person happy. But if that other person constantly thinks of what to do to reciprocate, the value of the gift is diminished.

We had another gathering of all the AFS students in Sandusky, Ohio. Each had two to three minutes to talk and explain what preconceived idea they had about life in the U.S. that has now changed. I mentioned my preconceived idea was based on the American movies, glitter and luxury. But now, I realized Americans go for comfort and practicality—whatever makes life more comfortable.

I have a lot of speaking engagements for the next three months and am truly busy. In March, I'm supposed to perform a Persian dance in the school talent show. The new room added to the house is almost finished and looks really nice. Mother, I won't say anything about the prom dress—you already know that it has to be floor length.

Hugs for all,

Manijeh

Two days later, Mom McClellan wrote to my parents. Of course my father had kept the letter. She is addressing them by their first name, no more formalities.

February 5, 1962

Dear Iran and Hassan,

Today it is very windy and cold and bleak here. I think a day like today is one of the worst kind—it is so grey and dull outside. Days when there is much snow are nicer, for it is bright and cheerful and the children love to play in the snow. I told Manijeh that she has probably experienced the worst of winter. I think she feels that it is not so bad after all. We have not had much snow this year.

It has been a good winter as far as our health goes too. None of us have been sick except for the cold Manijeh had at the beginning of the winter. I'm surprised that she has not been ill because of the great adjustment in food, living habits, climate, etc.

We all enjoyed the lovely pictures that you just sent. Jaleh is changing so fast and looks like such a lovely young lady. We are looking forward to her coming to the U.S. and staying with us some day.

When I bought gifts for Mehran and Cameron, Manijeh told me what size to get. But since I have seen their pictures, I'm afraid that she remembered wrong. They look like such big boys.

The young people of the church put on a play for the

women's club of the church tonight. Kathy and Manijeh were in the play—they enjoyed doing it and we women enjoyed having them.

All of the people who know Manijeh: teachers at school, the minister from church, friends of ours feel that she has made a very good adjustment to our way of life. The teachers say that she now seems much happier and more at ease in school than she did the first few months. I think her big problem is still the opposite sex. She tells us that in Iran a girl is not supposed to even speak to a boy. Here, of course, the girls are with the boys all day long and must be friendly or be considered a not very nice girl. So it has been a problem for her. But she is doing just fine.

It is late at night. Kathy, Manijeh and I are the only ones up. The girls both washed their hair. They are upstairs talking and giggling. I must go up and quiet them or they will wake up their father and the children. Kathy will be lost when Manijeh leaves.

All of my five children are supposed to make their own beds every morning—only one does—that is Manijeh,

> Love,

> Kate

P.S. Tell Jafar that Johnny Dollar doesn't need anyone to play "gangster" parts right now, but they can always use beautiful women like Mehri

Manijeh just told me that my Farsi looks like that of an elementary school student. The last time it looked like a kindergartener's. So I must be getting better!

February 10, 1962

Hello everyone,

Enclosed are bunch of photos of me skating on the frozen Lake
Erie. I'm not good at it, but I'm trying. The Polaroid photo
was taken at a basketball game. These games are a source of
entertainment for the community. Polaroid is when the picture is
developed right away after you pull the paper out of the camera.
The bad thing about it is that there is no film and one cannot make
more copies.

Mother's letter arrived and I thank you so very much for mailing
the prom dress. Funny you said at the post office they thought it
was a wedding gown! These speeches take a lot of my time. Last
night I gave talks in two places, came home about 10:00 p.m. and
then I had to prepare for a test in American Government class.
Dad McClellan helps me with my homework. He explained the
section on Income Tax, which is the hardest part in the American
government.

**I chuckled when I read this! Even today "Taxes" are hard to
understand and are subject to controversial debate!**

Today Tommy pretended to be sick and did not go to school. Dad
got angry with him and said, "If you are sick, then why were you
running and playing in the snow?" The real reason for him not
wanting to go to school was that he wanted to stay home and
finish up the homework he didn't do. It was some kind of project he
had to do since before Christmas. Today, Mom McClellan spent the
whole day helping him with the assignment.

Mr. King has written to AFS, New York and has explained my

situation and asked them if they agree he contacts some colleges on my behalf. There is a school in Dubuque, Iowa, that Mr. King graduated from and offers scholarships to foreign students. He wants to ask them about it. But of course it all depends on whether or not New York allows him to do so. I will keep you posted. Mr. King also asked if he could write to you. I was happy and told him by all means! Also mentioned to him not to worry about writing in English because you have translators and secretaries in your office who will translate.

George Washington's birthday is coming up—the first U.S. President—and with the weekend, we will have a four-day holiday.

Love,

Manijeh

February 23, 1962

My sweet sister, Jaleh,

I had no school today and had nothing to do this morning. I walked over to my friend's house (Judy Fischer), which is close by. They have just bought this house, and Judy wanted to paint her room. I helped her, and then we had lunch. Her sister, Jean, a really nice girl said hello to you and said she is looking forward to your letter. Their new address is: Jean Fischer, 176 Belmar, Avon Lake, Ohio.

Kathy and two other girls from Avon Lake had applied to AFS program to go abroad. Today, Kathy received a letter informing her that they can't find a family for her, so her application was rejected.

It is 23rd of February, 10:30 p.m. People are going crazy over the man who orbited the earth three times. He received a medal from President Kennedy. It was televised. Whatever happens here, it will be broadcasted over the T.V. and people all over the United States know about it. Because of George Washington's birthday, school was out on Thursday. They cancelled classes on Friday and then combined with Saturday and Sunday we have a four-day holiday!

The other night I saw a play in Cleveland with one of my classmates. **(I was on a date, but I'm not mentioning it in the letter!)** Kathy is at a concert with her friends, and it is snowing like crazy. I did cash Dr. Fayaz's check, but don't need any money now. Mother wrote and said if I need a shawl or cape to go ahead and buy one. For the prom I do need the gown, and boys usually rent their tuxedos. Based on what I hear, if the girls need shawls or capes, they can also rent them. It might sound funny to you, but that is what they do here. For a one time deal no one spends a lot of money to buy a tuxedo or pay for an expensive cape. I also received the boxes of pistachios, and have set aside a box for Aunt Gloria. This Aunt Gloria is very kind to me and spoils me!

I miss you very much, dear sister. When I get back I have so much to share with you. I hope my experiences will come in handy for you. I must admit, when I was in Iran, I was a bit shy and also vain and self-absorbed. Here I talk to people from different walks of life. I feel comfortable talking to people and have a good time. Of course, dear Jaleh, I cannot ignore the level of education of the majority of folks here. Why do you suppose America today is the biggest and the richest country on earth? It is all because of its people. If people are smart, good and kind, it elevates the country.

I do miss Mehran and Kamran very much. Don't forget to learn English. Give my regards to our parents.

Your Sister, Manijeh

Chapter Eight

March 4, 1962

Dear Dad,

The two boxes of tea arrived. After lunch I fixed my family a nice
cup of Iranian tea. Of course there is no samovar here and I cannot
put the teapot on the gas stove. Therefore, I thought it was not
properly brewed. Mom and Dad McClellan really liked the tea.
Did you send a box to Mrs. Newman, or am I to keep one for her?
Persian New Year is just around the corner; let me know the exact
time the New Year begins.

**Norouz, or Persian New Year begins the first day of Spring,
and is celebrated on the Spring Equinox. Sweets, new clothes,
time spent with family and friends, encouraging compassion,
wishing everyone peace, joy, tranquility and good health—
these are all part of the celebration of Norouz, which lasts
for two weeks, during which time schools and the majority of
businesses are closed. In Iran the festivities are not complete
without the Haft Seen, a table with seven objects that begin**

with the Persian letter "S." Family members gather around this table and watch for the precise starting time of Norouz, which is known in advance based on the published astronomical calculations. That is what I was asking my father to let me know, the exact time the New Year begins.

A few days ago, Mr. King called me to his office and read me the response he had received from AFS. It said, "AFS students have agreed that upon completion of their year, to go back to their own county and there is no exception. Manijeh's case might be exceptional in that when she goes back universities might still be on strike and closed. She can go to another foreign country after this year to continue her education."

This is the basic summary of the letter they sent Mr. King. However, Mr. King had already written to the president of the college in Dubuque, Iowa to inquire about scholarship, housing, courses, etc. He said he wants to write you a letter and I gave him your office address. I reminded Mr. King that although I'm a guest in this country this year and there is a lot of fun and games, but if it becomes possible for me to continue onto college, I'm not afraid of hard work!

I went to an ice skating show, the one we call *Patinaj*, dancing on the ice. The new room is finished and for the Persian New Year we are planning to invite my classmates, and have a tea party.

I gave a talk at the Kiwanis club. It is an organization for men and Dad McClellan is a member. Mr. King was also there. I showed my slides and they asked questions. A gentleman asked, "Are there any bald men in Iran?" I pointed to a bald man who was sitting up front and replied, "Of course, just like this one!" They found it hilarious.

Is there any snow in Tehran? It is sunny but cold here. Everyone likes the beige suit with the brown velvet collar Mother made me. They think it is elegant, and I'm proud and tell them my mother made it.

I have to write a research paper for my English class. My topic is, "Is it prudent to get married between the ages of 14 and 19?" I have to debate the subject and write about it. I have already collected a lot of articles. The use of library is very important here, and basically every six weeks we have to read at least one book and summarize it for the English class.

Thanks, father, for all your valuable guidance and coaching.

Your daughter,

Manijeh

33880 Lake Road
Avon Lake, Ohio
March 9, 1962

Dear Mr. & Mrs. Golbabai:

Thank you so very much for sending me the box of delicious tea. It was very thoughtful of you, and I appreciate it very much. We like tea a great deal, and as Manijeh has no doubt, told you, we do not have very good tea here. I do not know why this is so. My sister brings me good tea from Canada. I think she gets it from

England, but here our tea is not very good. So you can
understand why I am enjoying your gift so much. We also
like the can. It is so colorful and pretty. Our tea comes
in a box which is not at all pretty.

Manijeh is just lovely. Oh, how proud you would be
of her if you could be here with her. She has so many
friends and everyone speaks so well of her. When she
comes home you must have her give a speech to you as she
does here for the different groups of people. Wherever
she speaks she makes new friends. This is good for all
of us. It is good for us because we know that Manijeh is
happy with us; it is good for AFS because they know they
did the right thing in choosing Manijeh to come; it is
good for Iran, because Manijeh makes friends for Iran
wherever she goes. I think we can all see how we could
all get along better in this world if we knew a little
more about people all over the world. I hope you realize
and are properly proud of what Manijeh has done. It
cannot be easy for any girl to go into a strange home, a
strange land, a strange culture, and become at home. But
Manijeh has done it, and it has made us all so happy. We
always worry, and I am sure that you must worry too, that
exchange students will accept too much of the habits of
the country in which they are living for this year. But
you do not need to worry about Manijeh: she loves Iran
and is such a fine and loyal daughter of her native land.
She may seem a little too American to you when she comes
home, but do not worry, she will get over it. It seems as
if she can do everything well. I hope Manijeh likes us as
much as we like her. We want friends in Iran too.

As you know, our boys and girls go to plays and dances and other social gatherings by themselves without their parents being with them. For some time, Manijeh did not want to do this, and I do not think she approved of this practice. She has now gone to several affairs with some very nice boys and I think she now realizes that our standards are not so different from those she has been accustomed to. You need not fear anything; Manijeh is very trustworthy. We would not let her go with a boy whom we did not approve of. She seems to attract boys who are the kind that we would like to have her go with.

There will be a great deal of excitement from now on. Everyone looks forward to Graduation and there are many parties and plans to make. Soon, now, the winter will be gone and the weather will be nice and warm again. I do not think that Manijeh has suffered with the cold. We now forget that this is her first real winter, because the coldest weather is past. The rest will be much better. I will write to you again soon and let you know more about your daughter. We are grateful to you every day for letting her come to us this year.

Thank you once again for the gift of the tea.

Yours sincerely,
Mrs. John W. Newman

March 11, 1962

Dear Family,

I wish you all a Happy Norouz, and pray for prosperity for all.

I've not been sitting idle—I'm growing some wheat (Sabzeh) and it is sprouting nicely. Mom Mac said they'd never thought of growing wheat this way. I'm going to arrange for the "Haft Seen" and will give a party for my school friends, Iranian style. I'm inviting only the senior class—around 31 students. I will serve tea and cookies and play Iranian music.

Mrs. Newman has also received the tea. Mom Mac is surprised that you have not received the packages she sent, and Dad Mac jokingly said, "Maybe the ship carrying the packages has sunk!" and Mom Mac did not find it funny. Anyway, let us know when you receive them.

Mrs. Bomberger asked me if you have to pay custom duty on the gifts you receive from the U.S. I didn't know—so write me the answer, please.

I was on a panel discussion at a nearby town. Two other AFS students were present, a girl from Costa Rica, and a boy from Germany.

All of us seniors have been measured for cap and gown for the graduation. I recently saw a movie in Cleveland. It was a powerful court drama about Hitler's time, "Judgement in Nurenberg." It was about the trial of those who followed Hitler's instructions and killed so many Jewish people and gassed them in bathhouses. It was horrible. If they show it in Iran, you must go see it. (**The movie was shown in Tehran, and I actually went with my father to see it a second time.**)

Regards to all,

Manijeh

March 23, 1962

Dear Mother and Father,

Happy New Year! My best wishes for your health and happiness.

I haven't written for a while, because frankly I have so much to do that I hardly get time to do my homework. This past week, every night I had to give speeches and was up till midnight. That is why, when I come home from school in the afternoon, Mom McClellan makes me go take a nap and rest. We usually eat dinner at 6:00 p.m. Today, she borrowed a big round copper tray, I believe made in Turkey, and I'm to arrange the "Haft Seen" on that tray. But we only have five items with the letter "S" and not seven. I can't find "Senjed" and "Samanoo" here. But I do have the English Koran! At 4:30 p.m. the photographer will come to take some pictures while I light the candles.

Last week went to a luncheon in Cleveland—three American authors were presenting and talking about their books. One writer, Curtis Harnack, had taught English literature at the University of Tabriz for a year. I met him after the talk and he signed his book for me.

Yesterday I spoke with Mr. King. He showed me the letter he had received from Dubuque University. The content indicated they are willing, actually eager, to accept me. It is not a final acceptance, but they will write to Mr. King again. The only obstacle is AFS regulation. Mr. King said he would do anything he can to help me, and I do believe he would.

A little while ago a letter from AFS arrived, asking for my round trip travel ticket to be sent to them in New York. Mom McClellan promptly sent my ticket to them. Tonight I'm having a party for 30 of my classmates: tea and cookies.

I have to share something with you. When I first arrived, I kept a bunch of the little gifts locked in my suitcase. I asked the family to leave the house, so they went to Aunt Gloria's. Then I got busy and decorated the place with Persian paisley table cloth, copper dishes, decorative hookah, etc. When they came back, I said these are their Persian New Year gifts. For tonight's party I have made big flowers out of crepe paper, and they look really nice.

Norouz greetings to all the family members.

Manijeh

March 29, 1962

Hello Family,

Thank you for sending those beautiful Norouz cards.

Can't emphasize enough how busy I am. Last night gave a talk in Lorain, then I had to prepare a report for American Government and present it in class. Also had a test in English class. After lunch I was about to fall asleep. Mom Mac insists I take a nap when I get home from school which is usually around 3:30 p.m.

Turned out we had 34 people at the Persian New Year party! Fauzia from Pakistan and Eckart from Germany, both my AFS friends, came to the party and Fauzia spent the night at our house. "Haft Seen" on the table, Persian table cloths, paintings and posters made the room look very Persian. We served cakes, cookies, tea and Pepsi. A Pakistani young man who is a graduate of Michigan State University, works for a magazine called "Asian Students," which is published out of California, was also present at the party. He interviewed me and took some photos to have it published in that magazine.

Weather is turning really nice, it is Spring after all. Usually after lunch students go to the gym and dance. But today going outside was mandatory. A professional women's basketball team came to our school and played against our male faculty. They were hilarious! The guys lost.

If you have not received McClellan's package yet, it might have something to do with the postal situation in Iran. I will not have any speaking engagements beyond May—AFS forbids it.

Love to all,

Manijeh

Chapter Nine

April 11, 1962

Dear Mother, Father and Sister,

You are probably getting tired of me saying how busy I am here!

One of the teachers from school **(Mr. Turner)** and I went to Cleveland to listen to a lecture by Dr. Eric Fromm, the psychologist. The auditorium, large enough for 20,000, was packed and many sat on the steps in the aisles. Didn't know so many people were interested in psychology here!

I gave a talk to a group of Girl Scouts, and they gave me a necklace as a gift. Last night I was a speaker at the PTO (Parent Teacher Organization) of our school. They served desserts afterwards. So far I have given 30 speeches.

My family and I attended a gathering of foreign students from northern Ohio. It was not an AFS function, and I was the youngest of the group. Others were doctors, Ph.Ds, graduate students from different universities in the area. A young woman from Philippines performed an ethnic dance, and a doctor talked about hypnosis and actually hypnotized a gal who automatically picked up a broom and started sweeping the floor! Foreign students were mostly from Pakistan, India, Japan and Philippines. The Japanese knew less English than others. Some older men in the group had grants to come to the U.S. to visit for only two or three months.

I had sent Mr. Amini in Idaho a Norouz greeting card and yesterday received a reply. He said he was so shocked to receive my card, as if he was hit by lightning! He asked me to call him and let him know if I ever need anything, or need any money! His letter was full of praise of you and Uncle Jafar. He is married and they are expecting their first child in early summer.

Mr. Amini was a student of my Uncle at Alborz High School. He was from one of the provinces and did not have any family in Tehran. Uncle Jafar took him under his wing and helped him a lot, academically and monetarily. He was also hired to tutor me in English when I was in middle school. His goal was to work, save his money and travel to the U.S. He did just that and ended up in Pocatello, Idaho.

The weather has been really nice and most of our gym activities are outdoors. I stayed after school to participate in track. After one of my talks, I received $20 as a gift. I'm going with Mom McClellan to buy some summer clothes. I'm wondering when I will receive my prom dress! But I'm not worried.

Mom Mac said a few ladies have called to thank me for the talk I gave, and had mentioned I have slight resemblance to Elizabeth Taylor! Ha Ha. Really funny. I think it has something to do with my dark eyebrows!

I visited the Steel Mill in Lorain. It is huge, and I hope my country would have a factory like that.

Love & regards to the whole family.

Manijeh

April 14. 1962

Dear Mother and Father,

Believe it or not, despite all the work, I never get tired here! I exercise and enjoy good fresh air away from a big city. Actually most Americans try to live away from the big cities. My American Dad drives half an hour to Lorain and back every day. Everyone says the big cities with factories, offices, etc. are not suitable for living.

The prom dress arrived, as well as the packages of pistachios and Gaz.

Mom Mac had arranged them on the table when I arrived from school. Kathy and I first opened the box with the dress in it. It is beautiful. Thank you so very much! The bodice is a bit big, but Mom MCClellan said she would send it for alteration. I don't know where she can find a seamstress who can do this! The white silk flower will go well with the dress.

We all went to a school play last night, "I Remember Mama," Janet Newman has a part in it. After the play, Mrs. Newman came to our house to see my prom dress.

I was still sleep this morning when Kathy and Jane ran to my room yelling more packages have arrived! The mailman had brought them to the house. Wow! Thank you for the Baklava, the marzipan mulberries, honey-almond candies and more Gaz and Pistachios! Please don't send any more. I thank you, again. I intend to send a box of Gaz to Mr. Amini because he doesn't have anybody in Iran to send him these things.

Mom McClellan is asking a lot of questions about the packages you received from her, and I don't have the answers: Were the packages opened? Did you have to pay duty on them? Did Mehran and Kamran's cowboy boots fit them? And she is puzzled that Jaleh's slippers got lost. (I will bring her another one!)

The pictures of the Shah, Queen and the Crown Prince are all over the news here. Shah was speaking on TV, but I didn't see him.

Mom Mac has sent you a big Sears catalogue. They have all tried the Baklava, but I don't think they like it because it has some rosewater in it, and they think it smells like perfume!

Mrs. Newman and Mom McClellan have both received father's letter. But your letters are very formal and dry! Please tell your secretary not to translate your letters as if they were official business letters. These folks here are like my second parents, and when your secretary translates and puts all kinds of formal words and phrases, it does not have the informality and warmth that Mom McClellan sends in her letters. But don't worry, it is all part of the language problem.

Dad McClellan says he is going to gain weight because of all the sweets you have sent them!

Thanks again for all the goodies. Hugs and kisses for all.

Love,

Manijeh

April 19, 1962

Dear Mother and Father,

Last night Mr. Amini called from Pocatello, Idaho. Idaho is a long ways from here. It takes several days by train to go from Ohio to Idaho. He asked about my school, the program, and how long I would be here. He said he would send me a plane ticket to visit him, and said his wife will be very happy if I lived with them. I thanked him a lot, but he said I don't need to thank him, and that he will never forget the kindness and help you and Uncle Jafar have given him. He said I'm like a sister to him, and he would do anything to make it possible for me to continue my education in this country, even if he has to send me to Canada and bring me back. Said he would write you a letter to get your permission.

Mr. King showed me the letter he had received from father. He said rest assured of the acceptance to college; only if we could get AFS to agree and let me stay.

Mr. Sholevar also sent a letter saying I can call him collect any time I want to.

Please don't forget to send Thank You note to the McClellan's for the stuff you received, even if Jaleh's slippers were missing, and the cowboy boots for Mehran and Kamran did not fit properly.

School is about to end and I'm scheduled to leave Avon Lake on June 25th. We will travel by bus to the eastern states with the rest of the AFS students. Plan is for us to leave the United States at the end of July.

Mr. Amini called and said if I didn't want to remain under the AFS program, I could go live with them, and consider his house as my own home! He said I could apply to any college or university in Idaho.

Please do not worry about me at all; I'm healthy and happy and everything is going well here.

Today I was invited to have lunch at a nursing home, The Golden Age Group. These old folks were all in good spirit and laughed and joked a lot. I was sitting next to a very old gentleman. He must have been over eighty years old and was also hard of hearing. His napkin kept falling off his lap, and out of courtesy, I bent over each time and picked it up for him. He kept putting his hand on my thigh to thank me.

Easter is a religious holiday and it is coming up. We are planning to go to Michigan and stay at Aunt Mary and Uncle Jim's house. Mary is Mom McClellan's sister.

Regard to all,

Love,

Manijeh

April 25, 1962

Dear Father, Mother and Sister,

We left for Michigan on April 20th and it took us about five hours to get to Aunt Mary's house. She has five children and the oldest is in sixth grade. We had a fabulous time. Easter Sunday is when Jesus was resurrected. All candies and chocolates are egg shaped. We boiled a lot of eggs the night before which the children colored and decorated. After the kids went to bed, the grownups hid the eggs all over the house. Early morning, the children got up and carrying cute little baskets—which was prepared for them the night before—went around looking for eggs. This is a custom in the U.S. at Easter time.

On Saturday we had a tour of Michigan State University. It is a large and famous university in America. I can't tell you how vast and big it was. We visited all the buildings. The library has three floors; there are 25,000 students, which makes this place like a small city by itself. We visited boys and girls dormitories; saw apartments for married students, and saw the building for those who have already graduated but are still continuing. We saw the gymnasium, two covered swimming pools, and an indoor baseball court for rainy days. Girls mostly used their bicycles for going to classes in different buildings. We visited the college of education and its classes, which was most interesting to me.

We visited uncle Jim's brother in the evening. He is a Ph.D. student himself and also teaches at the college of education. His wife is Lebanese, and his mother-in-law had made some Lavash bread—they gave me some as a gift! There was another professor from Michigan State who has a doctorate in philosophy and teaches at the same college. We had the most interesting discussion about philosophy, psychology, Rousseau, and Hobbs, even Dale Carnegie and Alexander Dumas.

Father, the more I think about it, the more I find myself interested in psychology and education. Although I have studied natural sciences and my grades are good in physics, chemistry and other sciences, I'm not a bit interested in medicine. Unfortunately, in

Iran I cannot pursue education and psychology with a background in science. I just have to wait and see what happens.

By the way, I gave one of Kathy's classmates a haircut. It turned out well. Then Mom McClellan asked me to cut her hair, which I did and it turned out excellent. Then Kathy ventured and asked me to cut hers too. They are all happy with their haircuts. But I can't cut my own hair.

Daffodils are blooming and the weather is just beautiful.

Last Sunday was Dad McClellan's birthday. He is 40 years old.

Love to all,

Manijeh

Chapter Ten

May 3, 1962

Dear Parents and Sister, Aunt and Uncle,

I gave my final speech at the school auditorium for the entire school, for one entire period. The topic was family life, school and society in Iran. There are no more speaking engagement scheduled because graduation activities will begin.

AFS sent me the luggage tags. I will leave Avon Lake on June 25th for a bus tour to eastern states. On July 15 we will travel by boat to Holland (Amsterdam and Roterdam). Then we will take the plane to Athens and from there will fly to Iran. I'm sure the boat trip will be fun and interesting, as it is only for AFS students.

Since I have not heard from you regarding college plans and staying further, I am going to mail some winter clothes and books because I'm allowed only one suitcase on the bus trip.

Today, the senior class along with our English teacher went to Cleveland to see a Shakespeare play, and then had lunch at a restaurant. We had already studied the play *(The Tempest)* and tomorrow we will have a test on it.

We shopped for Kathy's prom dress. She bought a light green dress with fancy white gauze over it. It is pretty and I'm glad she found one that she likes. My prom dress is at the alteration—nothing major, just to take in from the waist.

It is amazing how wonderful the weather is. Everywhere is green, with tulips, narcissus, and blossoms on the trees. Oh, I also went to an opera in Cleveland. It was in Italian, was nice, but I fell asleep twice during the opera,

Last week the whole family went on a picnic at someone's farm. American farms are so different from the ones in Iran—the difference is like day and night. Farmers here have everything: tractor, refrigerator, and electrical gadgets for milking the cows.

American Government class is finished and we have started a unit called "family life." They showed a movie at school which I cannot explain to you now, but it made me very uncomfortable watching it. For boys and girls here, it was very normal. Americans are very open in discussing these matters and explain things very matter-of-factly.

The movie was about teenage physical intimacy between the sexes, reproduction, responsibilities, family life, and these kinds of stuff. It was uncomfortable for me to watch all that on screen with all the male students around, but noticed my classmates calmly absorbed the information.

Mrs. Bomberger sent me a graduation gift. It is customary here for friends and family to give graduation gifts.

Love,

Manijeh

May 11, 1962

Dear father,

Greetings and God always keep you as the protector of our family.

On May 8, 1962 at 2:15 p.m. I was interviewed on television. **I don't remember the name of the talk show or who had arranged for the interview. I assume it had something to do with all the news generated by the Shah and Queen's visit in April of 1962, and their meetings with the Kennedy's in Washington, D.C. And here I was, a high school kid who did not engage in politics.**

I have given 36 talks or speeches so far, and in all 36 I've been asked whether I'm engaged to anybody. When the interviewer asked me the same question, I was so frustrated that right there and then, with people watching, blurted out: "I don't understand why people keep asking me this question everywhere I go!" She snapped back, "Because you are an attractive girl." Anyway, they asked about Iranian women, schools and a bit of comparison between the two cultures. It lasted several minutes.

I received your eight-page letter, along with the response you had sent to Mr. Amini. This is what is happening: Mr. Amini called from Idaho and advised me to send a letter to the immigration office and let them know I'm a recipient of the AFS scholarhship, but now I have been accepted to a college and ask whether I can stay based on that acceptance. I've also talked to Mr. King at length who has all my transcripts. Mr. Amini wants me to send my transcripts to Idaho State College, and is sure they will accept me. My passport is now held by AFS in New York. I think Mom McClellan sent it to them. Amini thinks if I can get my passport back from AFS, I can easily go to Canada and then come back to the U.S.

Students sponsored by AFS program were on Exchange Visitor visa which had strict limitations on the time they could remain in the U.S. It would have been possible to transfer sponsor, get a student visa based on acceptance to a college, if I had my passport to go to Canada and then returned to the U.S. Looking back, I was not so keen on the idea and wanted to get back home.

Yesterday, a short letter came from Mr. Stephen Galatti, the head of AFS. It is such a short note that I'm copying the whole letter for you here.

Dear Manijeh:

Dr. Goudarznia came to see me yesterday in regard to your staying further into the year, but I had to tell him that of course you couldn't.

He is such a nice person and he understood our AFS obligation.

My best,

Stephen Galatti

Dr. Amir Goudarznia was the economic attaché to the Embassy of Iran in Washington, D.C. He was a friend of Uncle Jafar.

There you have it, father, the exact response from Mr. Galatti. So, it appears that Dr. Goudarznia had gone to AFS headquarters himself to talk to Galatti, unsuccessfully. As you also mentioned in your letter, they are very strict with the rules attached to this scholarship.

On the AFS bus trip I must have ONLY one suitcase and a handbag. I have a lot of books and winter clothes which I must send via surface mail. I repeat, I don't know if I will hear from the immigration office. In any case, my travel plans are all in order, set by AFS.

Everything is going well here. I have not neglected my AFS duties. I have finished all my talks, and am getting myself ready for the graduation. There is a lot going on. Looking back at all the stuff I did at school, all that I've learned about government, social life, American family, I feel my life experiences have doubled. One cannot explain everything in a short letter like this. Whatever I have learned, I hope to share with Jaleh and my cousins.

You mentioned about the University of Tehran and the fact that even with a science background, I could study language, literature or psychology. That is great news.

Anyway, I will do what I'm supposed to do— and really am doing my best. If it is meant for me to stay here, I will. If not, I will come back like all the other students. Maybe after I finish college in Tehran, I will return here for higher education. Since I know how to type, hopefully you will buy me a typewriter to use at home.

Fifteen more days of school left, and in two weeks we will have the Prom. Kids are beginning to decorate the school gym.

Trees are blossoming and tulips, daffodils and violates are everywhere.

Regards to Mother and Sister.

Your daughter,

Manijeh

May 22, 1962

Dear Father,

Yesterday, I heard from the organization that overseas Iranian
college students in the U.S. They said, as long as I have a passport
and a student visa and the organization that has sponsored me in
the U.S. (AFS) does not object, they are fine with me staying in this
country. They also sent me a form to complete and send back with
a photo. I could not answer two questions: my passport number
and the date of issue, because my passport is kept by AFS in New
York. I'm still waiting to hear from the immigration office.

Mr. King has received my transcripts which were sent to him
through the office of The American Friends of the Middle East. I did
as Mr. Amini suggested, I applied to Idaho State University, and Mr.
King had a copy of my transcripts sent to that school.

You asked whether the McClellan's and/or the Newman's would help
me. What kind of help are you referring to? It all depends on my
own initiative, hard work and motivation. Twice that Mr. Amini
called from Idaho to discuss my educational plans, I mentioned it
to my American parents. They disagreed and said I should not go
against what AFS says and must return to Iran. It is not that they
don't like me, they just want to follow what AFS has told them, and
what they have agreed to. They have agreed to have me in their
home for a year and that is it. They will do nothing more. And I
don't expect them to do anything more. It is not their responsibility.
If I want to attend a college here, I must do it myself, and sending
the transcripts is part of school's job. That is why I say Mr. King
has helped me a lot.

If it works out here, fine. If not, I will continue my education at the

University of Tehran and hopefully down the road, I will come back here for post graduate studies. I also want to mention that I read your letters at least three time! On page 179 of the book, *Extracts of Ideas*, it talks about patience! Please be assured I have learned how to be patient and am no longer the impatient and grumpy girl I was.

I miss you all. Please thank Uncle Jafar for the wonderful gift he gave me. I've taken many pictures with this good camera. Sending kisses to Jaleh; I'm sure she will always be successful. I know she is busy with her finals, but it would be nice, if she has the time, to write to Jean, who looks forward to Jaleh's letters.

Love,

Manijeh

Chapter Eleven

June 8, 1962

Dear Parents,

The graduation ceremony is over. It was held at the football stadium, and we all wore caps and gowns. Mr. King gave a summary of my biography, and what a good ambassador I've been for my country, and how much they have learned about Iran. He had asked me to stand up when he talks about me. I got my diploma. Mom McClellan had a graduation party for me—many friends and neighbors came over and brought me gifts.

About my college situation. In short, it is impossible for me to stay here. I had agreed to return at the end of the year and not come back to the U.S. for two years. What is the use of going to Canada for two years? If I could have come back to the U.S. right away, based on Mr. Amini's invitation, I would have done it. But not coming back for two years, it becomes very complicated.

Dr. Sholevar wrote and said he is leaving Pennsylvania and moving to New Jersey by the end of June. We are all very busy here. Kathy is getting ready to go to a Girl Scout jamboree in Vermont, and I'm getting ready for the bus trip, packing, wrapping, etc. On June 15 they are having a goodbye party for me.

I saw Uncle Jafar's picture in the magazine you sent. In the same magazine there was an article about the victims of the flood in southern part of Tehran. It made me cry, and Kathy said to me, "Why are you crying? There is nothing you can do; this can happen anywhere in the world." I guess she is right, but I was very sad.

Mr. Amini called again, and we said goodbye. His wife just had a baby boy; they named him John. He is also very busy with his own life. In short, everyone here is busy working and taking care of themselves and their families. I also heard about another scholarship for college here—but for now I have to wait two years.

Please don't expect too many letters from now on. I'm really pressed for time.

Hugs and kisses for all.

Manijeh

June 14, 1962

Dear Parents,

Wish you health and happiness, as always.

Yesterday, I received another package from you with more gifts. It was an unexpected package. I know that sending these, particularly by air, will cost a lot. Why did you do that? I'm very appreciative, but if you remember, I asked you not to send any more gifts. Of course I do realize your motive for sending these. There are folks here who have helped and taught me a lot during this year—they will be the recipients of these gifts. I certainly will show my appreciation.

Americans give gifts for many occasions: for Mother's Day, Father's Day, birthdays and Christmas. But they are also very careful with their money, and know when and where to spend it. In any case, I'm thankful for your generosity. Don't send any more pistachios. We still have some left. I don't eat them, but my American Dad likes them after dinner.

I will start packing soon. I will be leaving Avon Lake within a week.

I will see you next month. Enshallah!

Hugs and kisses,

Manijeh

P.S. Congratulations to my dear sister, Jaleh, for being number one in her graduating class!

And here is Mrs. Newman's last lettr to my parents the day I left Avon Lake.

33880 Lake Road
Avon Lake, Ohio
June 23, 1962

Dear Mr. and Mrs. Golbabai:
Today Manijeh left Avon Lake. I know that her trip

through the Eastern States of the United States and the
rest of her trip home will be a wonderful experience for
her. I know that she will be very happy to get home to see
you and her native land again. But we will miss her so
very much.

She leaves behind her so many friends, more than you
could possibly imagine, who will never forget her. For
years to come, Manijeh will be a part of our lives. Every
time we go to Euclid Beach we will remember Manijeh.
Each Christmas time when we are making our preparations
for our celebration, we will be thinking about Manijeh.
When Graduation time comes each year there will be many
who will think back to Graduation 1962, and remember the
sweet little Iranian girl who became so much a part of
our school. The girls in Manijeh's class at school will
be talking to their new friends in College next year
about the friend they have in Iran. We are happy that
Manijeh is going to have the many good times that we know
she will have on her trip, and being reunited with her
family, but we are so sad to see her go. It will take us a
long time to get used to not having her with us.

And so I personally thank you once again for letting her
come to be with us this year and to stay in our memories
forever. We have always known that it was a great and
wonderful sacrifice that you made when you let her come
to us, and we feel that we are making the same kind of
sacrifice when we have to let her go back.

I do not need to tell you again how much Manijeh
was respected in the school and the community. She
contributed so much. The talks that she gave on Iran
were much appreciated by everyone, and I do think that
we all feel that we know a great deal about your country
which we could never have known before. She made a very
good representative of your country, and I am sure you
should be very proud of her indeed. It seems to be a fact
that when we get to know each other, our differences are
not irreconcilable. There are, of course, differences
in culture, tradition, and habits, which is as it should
be. But an honest understanding and appreciation of our
differences as well as our basic similarities of purpose
in life can make life so much more pleasant on this earth
of ours. Manijeh has done a great and good job.

I hope some day it will be possible for us to meet. It
will not surprise you to know that we will all be looking
forward to seeing Manijeh again. We cannot possibly
say good-bye to her. But for now she will be busy with
her college life, and we may all have to wait. Until the
happy day comes when we can meet face to face, please
accept my thanks for all that you did to make this year a
most happy and interesting one.

Yours sincerely,

Dorothy E. Newman

**So thankful to my father for preserving Mrs. Newman's letter. Her
last correspondence with my parents basically summed up my
year. At the time, I was doing everything to the best of my ability**

to be a goodwill ambassador, respecting and understanding both cultures—keeping the old one and learning from the new one. I didn't know how I was being perceived by students and the faculty at school, or the whole community. But the fact that Mr. King, the Superintendent of the school, was doing everything he could to have me stay and attend college in the United States, gave me a clue that I was respected and liked.

June 26, 1962

Dear Family,

On June 23rd at 4:00 p.m. the McClellan's drove me to Cleveland. It was a sad goodbye because Mom, Kathy, Jane and I were all crying. Dad was somber and standing quietly. It took us half an hour to say goodbye to each other. Then I went home with Mr. & Mrs. Hallier, the family that was assigned to me. They have a twelve-year-old daughter named Michelle. They gave me a ton of stationary and stamps to write to anyone I want. They are slightly older couple and were most kind, gentle and generous. Michelle and I saw *West Side Story* movie together in Cleveland.

Before I left Avon Lake, I attended several "goodbye" parties. Mrs. Newman and Mom McClellan helped me with packing my suitcases. I've sent two suitcases to NY full of my stuff, winter clothes, books, etc. Can have only one case with me during the bus trip. AFS charges $9 to mail those cases. Mrs. Newman gave me a check for $18 as a gift and I promptly sent it to AFS, New York.

Dr. Sholevar called and asked if I could bring a necklace for his mother. I said I will be happy to do so. But two days later, a big box arrived within which were four more boxes! There was no way I could fit those in my only suitcase. With extreme politeness, I returned the whole box to him, as suggested by Mom McClellan. I don't even have room for my own stuff and have given bunch of my clothes to Kathy. He is probably going to get upset, but he had asked me to take only a necklace, now there are four packages—so much for Iranians and their words!

At the present time, I'm in Endicott, N.Y. We will visit New Jersey, Maryland, and Washington D.C. The family that is hosting me is hosting another girl from Malaysia, and we are roommates. Our bus is comfortable and air-conditioned. With more than thirty AFS students in our bus, we are certainly having a good time.

Your "Thank You" note to the McClellan's was appropriate and timely. My writing time is very limited, imagine I now have two families to write to: you and the McClellans. They probably expect some news or post cards while I'm travelling.

Jaleh, please let me know what you want me to bring for you. Whatever I can think of, I know we have it in Iran. For mother, I bought a pair of serrated scissors for her sewing class.

With love to all,

Manijeh

On July 4, 1962, Mr. Amini had sent another letter to my father indicating his dismay that things did not work out for me to stay in the United States.

Chapter Twelve

July 14, 1962

Dear Jaleh,

While I write you this letter, I'm on the bus going towards Canada. Within a few hours, we will leave the U.S. soil and board the ship. (*Seven Seas*)

You can't imagine how much I have learned and experienced this past year. The bus trip, visiting different families with variety of background and education along the way, has been enlightening and interesting.

Jaleh, this past year was unbelievable, but I must admit no place is like home and one's own country. I miss Mother and Father, and especially you. Before I left Iran, I didn't know how much I love you. Oh, I forgot to congratulate you on being the first rank student in your class. I'm very proud of having a sister like you.

Jaleh, this AFS is an excellent program. I didn't know I had the ability to adapt so well to different environments. That adaptability is very important. Every day being in a different family (on the bus trip) is not only interesting, but also a learning experience. I suppose I will be in Tehran on July 24th. I might look a little different, but inside me I'm still the same person.

We spent five days in Washington D.C. which is a beautiful city. We had a special program the last two days when 2,222 AFS students were gathered together—students from all over the world. Boys and girls from different nationalities, color and religion were all friends and were crying while saying goodbye to each other. Can you imagine, if all the people of the world were this friendly, we would never have wars or enemies!

My dear, how is your English? I bought you a dictionary with pictures in it. I cannot think of what to bring for Father and Uncle. I know they don't expect anything, but a gift will show that I've been thinking of them. When I think of ties, socks, shirts, etc. well they have it all. Anyway, I think this is my last letter, and then I will tell you everything in person. I will be on the ship for nine days, which I think would be a totally different experience. Work on your English—I think it would be wonderful for you to also participate in this program.

I wrote this letter just to you so that you know how much I love you. Please thank Homa on my behalf for helping you in math.

I hope Tehran is not too hot!

Looking forward to seeing you,

Manijeh

The *Seven Seas* was a vessel chartered by AFS to transport all the exchange students from New York to Europe in 1962. The ship made four stops and at each port some students got off. Le Havre, Southampton, Rotterdam, and Amsterdam were the ports I recall.

Just recently I did a bit of research on the amazing history of the *Seven Seas*. During her thirty-seven-year history starting in 1940, the *Seven Seas* was originally a standard C3 class cargo ship, and became a U.S. Navy ship during the war (*USS Long Island*). After the war, in 1948, she was purchased at an auction by a Swiss-based company and was named *MS Nelly*. She was rebuilt into a rather basic migrant ship to operate services to Australia. The accommodations were most basic, mostly dormitories, and two dining rooms with long tables. In 1953 she was rebuilt and upgraded into a two-class liner. That is when she was renamed *MS Seven Seas*. By then, she had 20 First Class accommodations, and 987 Tourist class spaces. She was chartered to Europe-Canada Line which was established to provide inexpensive student/migrant travel to Canada. The *Seven Seas* frequently operated Trans-Atlantic voyages to and from North America.

Thus, it was on this basic, no frill ship that I sailed along with my fellow AFS students from Montreal to Amsterdam, flew to Athens, and then back to Iran on July 26, 1962.

Epilogue

The End Of A Year

The 1961-1962 AFS experience altered my life and had an ever-
lasting effect on how I perceived United States of America.
That one memorable year, at the age of seventeen, under the
supervision and careful watch of a responsible organization,
and the love and caring of a decent family, taught me incredible
lessons in life.

Because of the commitment not to return to the U.S. for two
years, I gladly stayed in Iran—attended and graduated from
the University of Tehran in English language and literature.
I also got a part-time job to work at the branch office of the
American Friends of the Middle East in Tehran. This job gave
me the opportunity to gain a great deal of knowledge about
American colleges and universities, and the requirements for
attending one. It turned into a full-time job when I graduated,
and my last position was assistant to the educational counselor.

In that capacity, I had the responsibility of overall supervision for placement at American institutions of all our scholarship and graduate applications numbering more than 100 a year.

Six years later, in June 1968, I came back to the United States with my husband and my sister, Jaleh, who by then had graduated from high school. Jaleh did her undergraduate and graduate studies in the U.S. and eventually retired after teaching in the department of foreign languages at West Point Military Academy. My husband, Khosrow, completed his Ph.D. at Northwestern University, worked for two major corporations, and eventually retired from his own consulting business.

As an exchange student, places like Iowa or Idaho were only names I had heard from Mr. King and Mr. Amini. Maybe it was destiny that years later, my son was born in Iowa and I received my Ph.D. from the University of Idaho!

I have completed what I call the "AFS cycle!"

In 1981, while living in Boise, the AFS organization appointed me as a counseling representative for the southern Idaho and eastern Oregon areas. My experience as a Winter Program student from Iran to the United State had prepared me amply to be a counseling rep. In that capacity I got involved in fund-raising for the program, conducted orientation for the exchange students, and was responsible for solving family and adjustment issues. Then in 1983, I became an "AFS Mom" myself when we hosted Juan Jose Cruces from Argentina. Life is fascinating!

When I went back to Iran in 1962, a bit of me stayed behind in the United States. It wasn't my clothes, as I had once dreamed, that made me to come back! I had recognized and learned to appreciate what true American life was all about. I had experienced an actual family life in the U.S. and no longer believed what I saw on the big movie screen. As a seventeen-year-old, I could not quite articulate—though I tried through my letters to my parents—all that I understood, absorbed, and certainly felt. That one year in Middle America matured me in so many ways.

Since my return to the U.S. in 1968, I have kept in touch with the McClellans and have visited them in Avon Lake. Tom McClellan was the only member of the family who visited my parents in Tehran when he was a teenager. He also spent a year in Uruguay as an AFS exchange student. Sadly he passed away in 1991.

Dad and Mom McClellan both passed away in 2008 and 2016 respectively. The last time I visited Avon Lake was in 2015. Together with Kathy, Jane, and Ted we celebrated Mom's 92nd birthday. It was a bittersweet visit for me bcause Mom was in memory care and could not remember who I was. She held my hand and insisted that somehow she was supposed to know me, and that my voice was familiar. Kathy and Jane both live in Ohio and the three of us had some laughter and quality time together. Ted has moved away and currently lives in Florida.

I have deep respect and love for both my native and adopted lands. My only hope is that the traditions and values of each country be respected by all nations. This is how we plant the seeds of love, friendship and understanding on this planet earth.

HOW DID MY LIFE CHANGE DURING MY YEAR IN MIDDLE AMERICA?

The answer would be, "very dramatically!" In fact, because of that year, not just my life but also the lives of many around me have changed. It was the most seminal year of my life.

I was a sheltered, naïve teenage girl from Tehran, dropped suddenly in the middle of a culture where dating, co-ed dances, and sex education in school were normal. But I didn't drag my chin on the floor with horror, surprise or shock. I never judged, but opened my eyes, and tried to observe and learn. The emotional impact of this year was both intense and subtle. And I learned to adapt.

Not only did I have to deal with extreme cultural differences, I had to learn how to write and speak in English, pass exams, speak to large groups, give interviews to the media, get along, and maintain my own personal ethics and goals. I learned invaluable lessons from my host family, and received help from everyone in Avon Lake. They took me under their protective community wing.

Everyday brought its own new challenges. The slide presentations, and the talks I gave to numerous groups and organizations; the families I visited for dinner and carried on meaningful and educational conversations in English, and the food I had to eat with a smile, whether I liked it or not.

I learned time management, independence, responsibility and non-materialism, "Stuff" is just stuff, it's the people who really matter. I learned to be accountable and responsible for myself.

Wow! Did I ever learn all those in a hurry!

These lessons have stuck with me over the past five+ decades. In my teaching, parenting and grand-parenting I've tried to pass on some of these lessons.

Probably the most important lesson I learned is international awareness, and the ability to understand different cultures. No matter our superficial differences, most people are just trying to live decently, get along, feed, raise, and educate their families.

What an opportunity for teens to change the world! Thank you, AFS.

Manijeh (Golbabai) Badiozamani

Florida, August 2022

ACKNOWLEDGMENTS

As always, I'm grateful for the opportunities given to me on two different continents.

I'm thankful to my deceased parents for preserving these letters, without which this book would not have been possible. I owe special thanks to American Field Service student exchange program and the people of Avon Lake, Ohio for making 1961-62 memorable, and a valuable life experience for me.

I would be remiss not to give tribute to my toughest and greatest "life coach," my late father, Mr. Hassan Golbabai.

Some memories for Manijeh, 1961-62 by Janet Newman, class of 1963

Manijeh, thanks for asking us Girl Scouts, troop 202, to share our memories of you during 1961-62 when you were an exchange student thru AFS. You lived with the McClellan family in Avon Lake, Ohio, and attended the Avon Lake High School as a senior.

I remember that you visited my family home early in your year with us, and I took you upstairs to see my room. It turns out that on my bed I had placed a large stuffed animal—not a delicate teddy bear, but something more like a floppy plush dog. I hadn't acquired for myself, but maybe someone won it at a fair and gave it to me.

When you saw the stuffed dog, you exclaimed something like, "Why do you have a toy on your bed? Toys are for children!" I was taken aback; many of my girlfriends had stuffed animals, but then I realized you were right. It was an example of a cultural exchange that had never occurred to me before in my sheltered environment.

Speaking of sheltered, another more vague memory is that we Girl Scouts were preparing to go on an overnight "camping" trip to last several days. We were pretty coddled, and for us camping meant few hardships. One of our leaders turned to you and asked you if you would remember to bring feminine sanitary products in case you got your period during our outing. You were clearly embarrassed and at a loss for words. Apparently this was something you weren't used to discussing casually.

I'm pretty sure we double-dated at the Junior-Senior Prom that spring, and as I recall, your date was the late Jim Kettner. I have photos and slides of us in our lovely prom dresses. Recently, when I mailed a photo to you, I commented that we would never again have such small waists!

You brought a truly international, intercultural experience to our small town. You were brave in trying new things even though you must have missed your family and familiar understandings of "how things are done."

Much love, Janet

MEET THE AUTHOR

Manijeh Badiozamani is a literary non-fiction writer. She was born in Iran and has lived in the United States for over fifty years. She earned a PhD from the University of Idaho, taught at the college level, and published her first book, *Family Tales from Tehran,* in 2019. Her second book, *One Summer in My Life, A Memoir in Short Stories,* was published in 2020

She lives in Florida with her husband.

Made in the USA
Columbia, SC
07 June 2023

17718917R00107